# VOICES *from*
# BARROW AND
# FURNESS

# Voices *from* Barrow and Furness

## Edited by Alice Leach

The History Press

First published in the United Kingdom in 2008 by
The History Press
Cirencester Road, Chalford, Gloucestershire, GL6 8PE

British Library Cataloguing in Publication Data
A catalogue record for this book is available from the British Library.

ISBN 978-0-7509-4743-5

*Remembering Furness people:*
*Joan Grainger, Benjamin High, Katie Percy,*
*Danny Patterson and Sarah McAuliffe*

Typeset in 10.5/13pt Galliard.
Typesetting and origination by
The History Press.
Printed and bound in England.

# CONTENTS

# ACKNOWLEDGEMENTS

Barrow Civic & Local History Society is grateful to the following organisations: Barrow Borough Council for underwriting *Voices from Barrow and Furness*; Barrow Community Regeneration Company Limited, for a grant towards recording equipment; and Neighbourhoods Grants Panel for a grant towards transcription costs.

I would like to acknowledge the following who have helped to make this book possible in so many different ways: *NW Evening Mail* for permission to use a number of their photographs; Christopher Kelly for allowing us to use a photograph of his sculpture, 'The Spirit of Barrow'; Castle Fine Arts for 'Spirit of Barrow' images; Robert Brady, Director of T. Brady & Son, International Haulage Firm for supplying photographs and information; and to Graham Watkins for his interest and assistance. I am indebted to Marianne Buchanan, Communications Office from BAE Systems for giving permission to use photographs of the Astute Launch and to Councillor Terry Waiting for his help and encouragement. A big thank you to Peter Leach, Features Editor of *NW Evening Mail* for assembling photographs and for helping and encouraging me (his mother).

Thanks are due to all interviewees for giving their time to share their stories with members of Barrow Civic & Local History Society's Oral History Group. Those interviewed are as follows: Dorothy Latham, Anne Robinson, Mary Liddell, Margaret Burrow, Pat Chapples, Maralyn Grainger, Thomas Round, David Marcus, Danny Patterson, Benjamin High, James Dunn, David Gill, Mike and Vicky Brereton, Derek Lyon, Hazel Edwards, Ian Smith, Gordon Hall, John Hutton MP, Margaret Crawford, Betty Wilkinson and Wyn Dawson, Sean McCusker, Alan Wright, Arthur Evans, the Revd Allan Mitchell, Jennifer Billingham, Daniel Eccles and Georgia Drew.

Other contributors are the late Katie Percy, who sent a written account of her wartime work in Barrow, from her Southampton home, and Sarah (Sally) McAuliffe who died aged 103 in 2007. This lady's nieces provided facts relating to her long life, so many thanks to Agnes Crayston, Anne Tunn and Margery Morris.

Unfortunately, it has not been possible to include material from all of those interviewed, but their recordings and transcripts will be stored in the Civic Society's archive and may be used in a future volume.

I am grateful to members of the Oral History Group for giving their valuable time to the project: Irene Cutcliffe, Denise Dawson, Vanessa Allen, Barbara Hawkes and Janice Urry. A special thank you to Denise and Irene for helping me with proof reading and for attending countless 'brainstorming' sessions.

*Alice Leach (Secretary/Chair, Barrow Civic & Local History Society)*

# INTRODUCTION

In March 2006, Simon Fletcher, Commissioning Editor for Sutton Publishing, wrote to me asking if Barrow Civic & Local History Society would be interested in producing a new book on Barrow. Initially the committee declined, stating that they were totally committed to their new project, oral history, and this was proving to be very time consuming. Back came Simon's response: 'I wonder if at some point there will be a book in it?' After much discussion, the members of the committee decided to go ahead. Interviews took place between 2005 and 2007 and *Voices from Barrow and Furness* is the result.

The Barrow Civic Society was founded in 1985. Its objective is to inspire locals with pride in their environment. This is carried out by a programme of education consisting of lectures, books, articles, guided walks and tours, both at home and abroad. In 1990, the society added the words 'and local history' to its title.

*Alice Leach, 2008*
www.barrowhistorysociety.org.uk

Logo designed by Trevor Skempton,
Barrow architect, 1985.

'Spirit of Barrow' by Christopher Kelly, Walton Road.

ONE

# VOICES FROM THE WARDS

## Dorothy Latham

*Dorothy Latham was born in Barrow in 1908, the same year Walney Bridge\* was opened. During her forty years in the nursing profession, she has been a staff nurse, a district nurse, a midwife and a health visitor. She was interviewed on 25 June 2006.*

I started my training to be a nurse when I was 23 years old at the former North Lonsdale Hospital in School Street in 1933 and I was there until 1937. During that time, we worked on the wards for nine hours a day. We also had to attend lectures given by doctors: Dr Ronald, Dr Liddle, Dr Miller and Dr Carson.

When we were in training at North Lonsdale Hospital, we had to be very careful how we used the medical things, it being a voluntary hospital. [North Lonsdale Hospital opened in 1877 in School Street. When the new Furness General opened in 1984, it continued as a clinic until 1988. It was later demolished].

When we were taken on as nurses we were measured and we got new uniforms. By the end of three years, the wages were 7s 6d a week. I worked in Ward Six which was a new ward, the accident ward; it was across the hospital yard. Victims of road accidents came in as well as workers who had suffered from injuries in Vickers Armstrong's shipyard and the steelworks. And of course, the odd drunk on a Saturday night.

Our training days at North Lonsdale Hospital 1933–7, Balcony Ward 2. Nurse Farrell (left) and Dorothy Latham. *(Dorothy Latham)*

---

\*  30 July 2008 is the 100th anniversary of the official opening of Walney Bridge (as a toll bridge), by the Mayoress of Barrow. It cost £175,000.

I was once doing night duty there and the night sister rang from the hospital saying, 'Be careful, keep your door locked, there's a drunk in the yard'. I thought well that's happy isn't it, being on my own and all these patients in beds on the accident ward, so I got the most able man up. I told him the story and he said, 'All right, I'll take care of you,' so you had the patients protecting you.

There was another time when a drunk came in. My parents were going to Dalton for New Year celebrations and they found this man lying in the road by Ruskinville and they thought he was ill and they got worried, so they got the ambulance and they brought him to the accident ward. My parents phoned and said, 'There is a patient coming in your ward – we found him on the road.' When we got him in, in bed and that, well everything came up on the ward floor, so we made him clean it up and he was sent out the next day; he was drunk, not ill.

I worked at Conishead Priory for a few months with my friend. I was staying at Roose with my sister. We had to walk from Conishead Priory in the blackout. The soldiers were in Conishead Priory and we felt sorry for them for it was cold and draughty; they used to put the plug in the sink to keep the draught out. My friend

Nurses dressed for a children's Christmas party at North Lonsdale Hospital, 1934. Dorothy Latham is seated at the front on the left. *(Dorothy Latham)*

Conishead Priory. *(NW Evening Mail)*

and I worked there for about nine months, but we didn't like the matron, so we gave in our notices.

*Conishead Priory is now the Manjushri Mahayan Buddhist Centre. The present building stands on the site of a twelfth-century Augustinian Priory, originally founded in 1160 by Gamel de Pennington as a hospital for 'the poor, decrepit, indigent and lepers' of the Ulverston area. It was rebuilt in 1821 by Colonel Bradyll. In 1880 it became the north's largest hydrotherapy hotel before becoming a convalescent home for Durham miners. During the Second World War, Conishead Priory was used as a military hospital.*

## Anne Robinson

*Ann Robinson was born in 1922 in Cambridge. She attended university at the London School of Economics. She became a state registered nurse in 1956 and later a staff nurse. In 1958 she did her midwifery training at Barrow and Blackpool, becoming a state registered midwife. Anne was interviewed on 20 November 2005.*

After I completed my midwifery training I came to Risedale Maternity Home, first as a staff midwife in 1959 and then as a sister. I was seconded from Risedale in 1965 to do the midwives teacher's diploma so that I could train the pupil midwives at Risedale and I continued there until I became matron. Nursing covers all branches of care, adults and children. After training as a registered nurse, I still had to act on doctors' instructions. Once I had done my full midwifery training, I was entitled to practise in my own right. I could care for and deliver a baby without calling for

Nurses at the entrance to the new Labour Ward of Furness General Hospital, Dalton Lane, Barrow. The first patients were admitted 14 October 1984. Back row, left to right: Madge Riley, Helen Higginson, Susan Wright, Maureen Bell, Jean Dockerty, Anne Robinson, Miss Fish (manager), Maralyn Poole. Front row: Pam Atkinson, Martha Cotton (deceased), Jean Asbury, Jenny King. *(NW Evening Mail)*

medical aid; unless, of course, there were difficulties. Care throughout is always the same really; it is basically to have a healthy baby and a live and healthy mother, able to care for her baby in a very satisfactory manner. Midwifery does consist both of the active caring for the patient or the mother and also the training, and teaching her the various aspects of parent craft, including nowadays, family planning.

Towards the end of my time at Risedale, I saw more than one generation become mothers. Many mothers would greet me with, 'Do you not remember me, Sister? You delivered Mary Jane.'

There were many changes throughout the whole system during the years I was nursing at Risedale, mainly because of the social changes that were occurring within the country as a whole, not just in the hospital or health services, but generally. A much freer atmosphere. When I first went to Risedale, a mother was kept strictly in bed for at least five days; she was not allowed home for ten days. The baby was cared for in the nursery and she had some training with looking after it but not very much. By the time I left, many mothers were up within a few hours of having the baby, and went home from twenty-four hours to the full ten days. This was pre-booked and should always be pre-booked, because it is important that the care continues so that as time progresses, mothers didn't just come into Risedale, they were also cared for in the community for the last period of their post-natal care.

Risedale Maternity Home, Abbey Road. The building was originally called Risedale Villa and was built in the 1870s by Joseph Rawcliffe. (Cumbria Record Office, Barrow)

The opening of the Risedale Maternity Home. *(Cumbria Record Office, Barrow)*

Some changes were medical; there was increasing use of diagnostic equipment which, of course, meant that any abnormality could be soon picked up. There was a much more active delivery programme. You often heard of mothers who had laboured for days and days in the past, but that ceased and it was felt a disgrace to allow a labour any undue length. Another change, of course, was in the visiting. When I first went to Risedale, husbands were allowed to visit only after the baby was born. By the time I left, husbands or fathers were present during the labour and were in the labour ward with the mother, staying there even when the baby was born. Sadly, we had to scoop a few of them up off the floor, but this was their right and they did come, and they did stay. Also, when the mother had had the baby and was back in the ward, her children were allowed to visit. This was a very new innovation. Many people were concerned that there would be a great risk of infection, but this in fact did not occur, and of course, it meant that mothers settled much more happily.

*In 1921 the building opened as Risedale Maternity Home. In addition to maternity work, arrangements were made for the treatment of cases of atrophy and debility in very young children. The Home was in the charge of Miss H. Pirie who was fully trained and possessed the Certificate of the Central Midwives' Board. There was a staff of qualified nurses. The Maternity Home closed in 1984. Risedale Retirement Home purchased the building in 1986 and a retirement home opened in 1987.*

## Mary Liddell

*Mary Liddell was born in 1924 and from a very early age, her ambition was to be a nurse. Mary was interviewed on 9 August 2006*

My training was from 1942 to 1945; half-way through, because the war was on, we all thought we would be sent to the front. In actual fact, we were sent to Conishead Priory. There were all the forces represented: Italian and German prisoners of war as well as our own men, who were all badly wounded. The VAD (Voluntary Aid Detachment) was not really trained; the Red Cross nurses might be doing war service, but any actual drugs had to come from the medical staff. Penicillin was like gold and we had these men coming straight from France who had not had their wounds dressed. The penicillin was measured each day by a colonel/specialist and was painted on wounds, not administered by injection; it was miraculous. Some of the men had lost limbs because of infections.

The wards were like army huts with forty men in each ward. We lived in billets. I can remember a German who had an abscess that was due to be lanced, but he insisted he did not want an anaesthetic because he was afraid of giving away secrets to the enemy.

After the Second World War ended I went to North Lonsdale Hospital to finish my training. We had to clean the wards; we pulled the beds out in the morning and we did the locker tops. The lockers had to be pulled out and nurses had to clean the wheels of the beds with turpentine. Dr Liddle wouldn't allow any ward sweeping for at least an hour before dressings were done and he used to leave a disc on the desk and if there was any dust he would know because it would settle on the disc. It was much cleaner then, and I felt satisfied when I knew the place was clean. There was a porter who used a polisher called a dummy that he pushed along; it was too heavy for the nurses to use. There were thirty-eight patients in the long wards. We nurses were never allowed to wear rings in case they got caught on one of the patient's wounds. For night duty we wore galoshes and carried torches; our desks were in the middle of the ward so everything could be seen and so that if somebody wasn't sleeping, we would know and we would make sure the patients were comfortable and had a drink. The food was atrocious! We had rations, for instance, one inch of sugar in a jam jar.

Mary in her nurse's uniform.
Jennifer Billingham is Mary's
daughter. *(Mary Liddell)*

North Lonsdale Hospital. *(NW Evening Mail)*

In the post-war years there were diseases such as scarlet fever, diphtheria and many cases of TB (tuberculosis). Streptomycin cleared TB, and I can remember a health visitor called Miss Wignall who used to visit patients in their homes to administer the drug. There was an infectious diseases hospital in Devonshire Road. An outbreak of polio occurred in the 1960s; an iron lung was used as treatment when patients couldn't use their own lungs. This rather primitive instrument looked like a long tube where the patient's head was at one end and there was a glass dome over it; you could see the whole body and the lungs working. The big problem with the iron lung was when the time came to take the patient off it, and this was crucial, very few could get off it and some were left paralysed. I remember the death of one fourteen-year-old girl.

Although the National Health Service came into being in 1948, pay and work conditions only improved slowly. I have worked as community nurse and as a hospital voluntary nurse, dealing with heart and stroke cases and sufferers from Parkinson's disease. To me, nursing is a vocation and unless you really love the job, you just couldn't and wouldn't succeed – and be fulfilled.

# TWO

# CHARITY WORKERS' VOICES

## Margaret Burrow

*Margaret was one of nine children. She was educated locally, and after leaving school, she worked for a chemist before qualifying to be a teacher. Owing to a spinal injury, she had to give up this work and some years later formed the Barrow & District Council for the Disabled. She is now Honorary Secretary of the Barrow & District Disability Association. Margaret was interviewed on 31 July 2006.*

I was born in Barrow at 30 Devonshire Buildings (the country's only remaining tenements), which are now listed buildings. I've lived in Barrow all my life, as did my parents before me. I have four brothers and four sisters and all but one, live locally. I've got lots of nieces and nephews; at the last count it was 250 relatives. A real Barrovian family, and I'm proud of that – I'd fight for the cause of Barrow to the death.

My mother struggled with nine children. I went to St John's Infant and Junior Schools. I passed the eleven-plus for the grammar school, but I couldn't go because Mum couldn't afford the necessary expenses. I was absolutely broken-hearted. I went to Alfred Barrow Girls' School which was a very good school, very disciplined. The headmistress was Miss Whyte and she was a lovely lady – all the girls respected her. I learnt a lot of things, especially about housekeeping. I was sorry to leave school. I could have transferred to the grammar school and gained qualifications, but once again there was no way Mum could afford to send me.

My first job was in a dry cleaner's shop and then I left there to work in Murray's Dispensary on Rawlinson Street. We worked fifty-two hours a week. We had to remember thousands of products and where they went, and that wasn't including tablets. We used to make the medicines; we had massive carboys and containers. When the children came in, I used to give them some glycerine pastilles. We sold Indian Brandee – that cured lots of things, and Fiery Jack. This was in the '60s, and we had medicines with dates from 1900. One we used was sixty years old, but it was a syrup and that doesn't go off. Chemists in those days were very different from what they are now. We did dressings; if people had wounds they came in and we dressed them – if they were bad we would send them to hospital. That stood me in

Margaret was awarded the MBE in 2002 and the League of Mercy Medal in 2006 for her work with the disabled people of Furness. (*NW Evening Mail*)

good stead for my work today. Every week mothers used to bring their babies in to be weighed. You had to have a good memory with a chemist, because you had to remember where every product was, on all three floors. It was a wonderland, all those little boxes, little mahogany drawers, with all sorts in and we had to remember everything that they contained. I worked at Murray's Chemists until I left to get married and have my two daughters.

When my youngest daughter was three, I went to college to be a teacher. I did the training in Barrow because there was a pilot scheme in operation in the town run by Loughborough University to train people to become teachers. After four years I gained qualifications in advanced fashion design and dressmaking. I taught my students dressmaking, millinery, crafts – all sorts of things, and I loved the buzz of education, and I had some wonderful students. However, it wasn't easy having a husband, two children, a house to run, and parents that were ailing at the time.

I struggled for many years with spinal problems. I was extremely thin in those days and didn't get much rest and I ended up disabled. I was advised by the medical profession that things were going to get worse unless I finished teaching. I had to follow their advice but it broke my heart. I went through lots of spinal operations and treatments, and adjusting to life in a wheelchair.

Eventually I had to sell my home and move to a bungalow. My younger daughter was at Park View School aged twelve, and my other daughter was at the Sixth Form College, ready to go to university. For about seven years, I spent a lot of time being involved with things, but feeling very sorry for myself. Then, one day, I decided I was going to do something about this. It just coincided with a group of pupils and professionals saying there was a need for a disability association in Barrow. This was for me – it was manna from heaven. We formed the Barrow & District Council for the disabled. We had little groups, action groups, where we would try and campaign for dropped kerbs and sports' facilities, things like that which, twenty-five years on, we are still doing. We had guest speakers and a telephone advice line, with one of us always on duty, and two other people in our complex with a telephone helpline. All of this helped me to come to terms with my disability, because I realised there are lots and lots of people in this town with similar problems, and we were, and are, able to help them.

I had a working life again, and as time went on, our executive committee, of which I was part, decided there was need for a base from which to operate, for people to have a drop-in centre just to have a chat. After consultations with colleagues, a business plan was drawn up. An application to the lottery was made for a massive grant to go towards suitable accommodation and the employment of staff to develop activities and services.

I called upon lots of people to help me with my voluntary work. I've always been able to phone a Barrow Island person and say, 'I have this problem, have you any idea what we could do about it?' and they've always been able to come up with a good solution.

We decided, as well as the telephone service, that there was need for an advice shop; we now have that downstairs. People come in for a whole range of things; for instance, enquiries about how to get a blue badge. On more than one occasion, people who have had only one month to live have asked for our help and we have helped them sort things out. We felt very privileged to help these people; the families were grateful and said we had made a big difference.

We got some money from Comic Relief, and we decided to start a computer service and it was then that we discovered what was available for ordinary people and what a limited choice was available for the disabled. Our highly successful computer project is now in its fourteenth year. Last year we had 1,100 students here learning to use computers on all different levels – basic to advanced. It is physically difficult for disabled people to go to college and it's rather intimidating. For these reasons we've set up our own night school type classes. At first it was just in the evenings because of lack of space, and now we have them during the day – morning, afternoon and evening. Last year, 1,600 students came to us. We have a membership of 2,000 and it's growing daily, and that is only the tip of the iceberg.

# BARROW AND DISTRICT DISABILITY ASSOCIATION
## The Margaret Burrow Centre

Writing on stonework of the Disability Centre. *(Graham Watkins)*

There are about 18,000 disabled people in Barrow; that's not really high for a town this size; it's about the national average. It's partly due to the heavy industry causing people to have asbestosis, asthma and so on. Barrow grew rapidly from a small village and people came from all parts of the country and generally lived closely together in family communities. They tended to inter-marry, not close relatives such as cousins, but often distant relations. This led to some genetic diseases; there are quite a lot of people with Friedrich's ataxia, and this is a genetic problem. If two people marry who both carry the gene, then the children are at risk from this disease.

So, there was a great need for the development of these four buildings which, to my surprise, they have named the Margaret Burrow Centre. Although I was sad to give up teaching and all the things I used to do, I feel I have a purpose in life. There's still so much we still want to do. Of course, there were so many people who have worked and helped to make the centre what it is. Some are no longer here and I remember them all.

# Pat Chapples

*Pat Chapples was born in 1955 in Askam-in-Furness. She attended schools in Askam and Dowdales Comprehensive School in Dalton. She is Project Manager for the Furness Homeless Support Group, situated at 27 Bath Street. This is a registered charitable organisation offering support, advice, resources and advocacy for people with accommodation related problems in Barrow and the Furness Peninsula. Pat was interviewed on 13 March 2007.*

After I left school, my first job was at the Kay Shoe Factory in Askam where I was a trainee machinist. Some years later I met and married a Brazilian gentleman and went to live in Rio de Janeiro and subsequently came back with my daughter, Natalie, to live in England.

I first became involved in helping the homeless in 1990; I was attending Furness College, taking some part-time courses and got very interested in doing some community work. I met some people who had just set up a homeless type of drop-in shelter that was based in Hartington Street in a Portakabin, and from there, it just sort of evolved.

Our organisation was at first connected with Community Action Furness and then we were very successful in getting a Lottery bid to actually buy and renovate the premises that we are now in, here in Bath Street. Furness Homeless is now a separate, independent charity, registered in its own right, and has been since 1995; our totally audited accounts are separate from any other organisation. We are fully independent and self-generating via our charity shop.

Project John is another housing charity that deals mainly with young people from the age of sixteen to twenty-five; whereas Furness Homeless deals with all age groups, both male and female, from the age of sixteen to possibly seventy plus.

In my experience of working here, we see lots of different people, many and varied, for whatever reason. We do have quite a big problem in the area being that there is not enough rented accommodation that is acceptable, and the rents are very high at the moment and therefore a lot of people find themselves homeless for whatever reason and that's where we come into play.

The main reasons that people come to us are because they have been evicted from the property because of rent arrears, break-up of marriage, family breakdown, domestic violence, or they can no longer afford a mortgage, and they get the house repossessed. Family breakdown is one of the biggest problems in the area we are dealing with; people often just don't get on with each other and that's when they end up at Furness Homeless.

We find a lot of people come from out of town to work in the Lake District in catering, and when the season is over they can no longer find employment. If they work in a hotel, they have a job and they live in, so when that job is finished, they have no home and they don't often want to go back to the place where they came from, which could be anywhere in the country.

The homeless people who come to Barrow usually have some form of connection with the town; either their father might have worked at the shipyard, or they may have come here on holiday to visit the Lake District. They feel they have an affinity with the area and its beautiful surroundings.

We do annual stats which show that we could see up to about twenty-five people a month; these are the people who are going to be evicted and become homeless, who could be sleeping on the streets – not always visible in Barrow. People say we never had any homeless people until the Homeless Shelter started, but that's the response to people being homeless, not the other way around.

We have currently about twenty volunteers working for us; sometimes it could reach twenty-five and that covers all areas of the project: the day centre, the kitchen facility, the charity shop and the collections service. In the past we used to deal with a lot of the churches and many retired people, such as retired teachers used to help, but that seems to have dwindled and now it seems we are dealing with a much younger group in all areas; in the day centre and our charity shop which is quite popular with the younger community.

The charity shop was set up as a response to people donating furniture, clothing, all sorts of bric-a-brac, things needed in kitchens, and we used to do car boot sales and I actually set these up myself. Then I went off to university so I couldn't continue with this work. A local businessman came to the rescue, the late Jimmy Vince. He let us have the ground floor of the building adjacent to here, 25 Bath Street, in order to run a charity shop. Then we acquired no. 23 Bath Street and moved our charity shop there. We then concentrated on no. 25 to create accommodation, so that's how the charity shop was set up and it actually raises a substantial amount of money to enable Furness Homeless to run, as well as providing furniture, clothing and personal items for the people that we house.

It's a community based shop that lots of people use, especially those who don't go very far – they walk up and down Bath Street calling once or twice a week, asking questions such as: 'What's Mrs So-and-So doing?' It's quite a community orientated place, very jovial, very nice; we've just recently renovated it with new windows with a donation from the council and we have central heating. It is updated and is a more pleasant place for people to come in and socialise.

Furness Homeless has two projects, although they run into one. We have five units of accommodation here at 27 Bath Street and four units of accommodation at 25 Bath Street which gives a total of nine. If we have a place available and a person is homeless and sleeping on the streets, we would try and provide accommodation here, but if that's not possible, we will liaise with other housing providers such as the council, other projects in the area, Silverdale Street Hostel or Project John, and also we would contact private landlords in the area.

When people come here to be housed, they move into 27 Bath Street, which is fully supported accommodation with support workers sleeping over in the evenings and they then have an allocated support worker who is based in the day centre. When they are able to move on to semi-independence and there is space available, they then move into no. 25, after which we look towards permanent accommodation in the community, which is fully independent living but has the back-up of our re-settlement plans. We provide them with all the things that everyone needs such as a cooker, bedding, furniture. We then go and visit them in

Pat in her office in Bath Street where she is Project Manager for the Furness Homeless Support Group. *(NW Evening Mail)*

their own homes, quarterly, or whenever they need it, just to make sure they are managing their budget and they are keeping on track with their lives. It may take twelve months or it may take two years.

Some people have been very successful and they have moved on to full-time employment and maintained the tenancies for more than twelve months. We've had quite a positive response in the last year for people have secured and maintained their tenancies, which is our aim – to put them into sustainable accommodation.

Our biggest concerns are for those people who come to us with medical, mental health, drug- or alcohol-related problems. Some of the homeless may also be ex-offenders so they have all these stigmas to overcome when they are trying to re-integrate themselves into the community. The sad thing is that some people can't move on at that particular time of their lives.

I'm sorry to have to say that homelessness has actually increased over the years I've worked here. The government has tried to get homelessness to zero but I don't think that's a viable option at the moment because there's no affordable housing; people need a home, a job – all the trappings that go with it and it's not out there. However, if we hear of anything and we can help a little bit along the way, we will always do our best to assist the homeless. To successfully house people gives me great satisfaction, especially when they come back and say, 'I've got a job, and I've met someone, and life is wonderful'.

## Maralyn Grainger remembers her mother, Joan Grainger

*Maralyn was interviewed on 8 June 2006.*

My mother, Joan Grainger, was born in 1929 in Barrow. She didn't have much schooling until her senior years, because as a young child she had suffered with meningitis and other ailments. When she left school she worked in the market for Allen's stall, packing biscuits to start with. After that she worked in the Co-op in Greengate Street. She studied confectionery to a very high standard, decorated wedding and ornamental birthday cakes. She did ballroom dancing up to gold medal standard. She was a good dressmaker and embroiderer, with an interest in the fine arts.

A big turning point in her life was when she joined Friends of Furness Hospital which had been formed in 1967. That came about because Dad had had a serious accident in Australia and she helped to raise funds for the local hospital and to help them build a facility for intensive care patients so they had some form of refuge away from the ward.

Then Mam had a brainwave. She decided it would be a good idea to restart the local carnival in aid of the local hospital. Many years previously it had been the

Joan shaking hands with the Queen. The occasion was the official opening of Furness General Hospital, 24 May 1985. *(Maralyn Grainger)*

Hospital Parade and it had been Infield Convalescent Home Parade, so after a few phone calls, it started off and grew and grew. There had not been any carnivals from 1958–70.

Mam became Chairperson of Friends of Furness Hospital and she was involved in organising the carnival parades for twenty-five years, the first one in 1970.

There was a procedure for choosing the carnival queens; selections appeared in the *Evening Mail* to start with, then they would have a dance where they picked out the five finalists – for the queen and her ladies in waiting. The dances were held in the Old Public Hall and then Forum 28. One year it was the Cemetery Cottages Club.

I made the costumes for the carnival queen float, except for the first four or five years. This was always a showpiece. It was a big undertaking but I enjoyed it. Mam did all the flowers and Dad all the backdrops – he got roped in and he became the Vice-Chairman of Friends of Furness Hospital. In the carnival's heyday, there were about 150 floats.

I remember one year Mam came up with this idea of swans for the main attraction on a float. The swans were wired together and we spent weeks filling them with toilet paper and tissue paper and then Mam decided we would take the carnival queen to Barrow Park to take some photographs, but the real swans didn't like us very much, so we got chased round the park with the carnival queen holding her skirts up, someone trying to feed the swans a packet of crisps, me with the robe and crown in my hands, and the photographer going in the opposite direction. That particular queen now lives in Bowness and won't go near the lakeside.

One year the navy decided to do a mock-up of a local submarine and they ended up soaking the mayor. The captain of the boat who was later to become a rear admiral, was summoned to meet my mother again and he said he'd never been so frightened in his life and he had to go and apologise to her for his sailors soaking the mayor in his robes.

There were other memorable floats: the bogey girls from Vickers' Shipyard always put on a fantastic one. The shop steward was Betty Jones and one year they did 'Coppernob' (Furness Railway engine number three). Hours and hours of work! People from the Derby Hotel in Dalton Road were experts in Disney ones and there were the baby floats. One year the Boy Scouts did a dragon that went winding round the streets till it caught its head on the overhead wires and blew a few flames that no-one was expecting.

In the days when we used to go past North Lonsdale Hospital, we arranged that they stopped outside; each troupe would stop to dance for the patients for they were able to bring them out in those days.

The carnival route was as follows: it started in Duke Street by Ramsden Square near the library, went up Abbey Road into Park Avenue, down Greengate Street along Rawlinson Street to Albert Street to the hospital into Church Street, back up Schneider Square down Duke Street to the starting point.

Collection boxes were given out and numbered – they had to be signed for, as you filled them and when you took them back, your number was crossed off and signed in. Only about sixty or seventy boxes went missing in twenty-five years. At the end of the carnival there would be a big wagon waiting to take all the tins to the

Joan with ten of her carnival queens. Left to right: Tracey Johnson 1990, Pat Sim 1974, Linda Parsons 1973, Vicki Richardson 1971, Janette Ley, 1975, Lorraine Emerson 1976, Joan Grainger, Yvonne Hawksworth, 1985, June Gow, 1984, Christine Adair, 1975, Paula Thorburn 1988. *(NW Evening Mail)*

bank, counted and put in the bank vaults till the next day. £7,000 in loose change! In the early days before we got to use the bank, it was in Mam's front room and we had police cordons round the house.

Some of the carnival queens in later years thought that it was all a bit of a joke, until they went round the hospitals on the Sunday. To be honest, the five girls who set off on the Sunday mornings weren't the same girls who came back in the evenings; they had learnt an awful lot and everyone without exception had enjoyed the experience and learnt that the older generation required some care and attention and needed to be treated like human beings.

We used to go to Basterfield House and there was a resident there who used to come out with a poker and we had to 'knight' him before we were allowed in. We would go to Ostley House for the blind. We used to let them smell the flowers, feel the materials, describe the colour of the dresses, the texture of the fabrics. There was one old lady there whose language was very colourful, but apparently when the doctor came round she was all sweetness and light, but when we got there she uttered words nobody had ever heard before. Mam got all this on video which she played back to the doctors. The carnival queen said, 'We've come to see you' and she told her in no uncertain terms where to go.

One time we went to Roose Hospital and this old man was asleep and when he woke up all these girls were round his bed; it was Queen Elizabeth II's Silver Jubilee Year and the girls were in white and silver and then he woke up and he thought he had died and gone to heaven with the angels. He was most disappointed when he found out it was just five girls dressed up.

The carnival took up all of Mam's time; she thoroughly enjoyed doing it, she seemed to have the gift to turn things into successful events. She cared about what she did and as I said before, she had her own personal reasons for wanting it all to come into fruition.

Mam instigated the building of the bungalow in the grounds of Furness General Hospital in Dalton Lane. This was built as a facility for relatives of seriously ill patients to give the opportunity to get away from the ward, to have a shower, make themselves a meal, relax, watch television for a little while. If they were needed, the hospital would ring, so they could go back over. Judging by the comments in the book that we had, people very much appreciated the bungalow which is called Kirvin House after Mam, her maiden name being Kirvin. Mam's father had been a builder. Mam was in and out of the bungalow quite regularly, usually to support anyone who happened to be there. She would turn up with biscuits and sandwiches to persuade those who didn't feel like eating. It took up most of her time.

Mam had to attend many meetings. She was also a member of the Community Health Council which was the watchdog for the hospital. Altogether, Mam helped to raise a quarter of a million pounds for the hospital.

Mam used to decorate the Christmas tree at the hospital and do seasonal decorations for the chapel. She'd be up there till midnight some nights; she would take a tape recorder with some nice quiet music that she would sing to while she did the flower arrangements. In fact, the last one she did was while she was a patient when she was ill. She was ill for nine months before she died in St Mary's Hospice, Ulverston, in 2003.

In 1998, Mam had been awarded an MBE by the Queen for her work with Friends of Furness Hospital. My father and daughter, Laura, went to Buckingham Palace. Afterwards we went to the Savoy and the waiter there was built like Pavarotti and he got down on one knee and serenaded Mam. Laura was only six at the time but she remembers the day and enjoyed it. Mam was very proud; she was a Royalist anyway. I don't think she realised the award was in appreciation of her work. She just thought that it was something she wanted to do and didn't think she should get something special for doing it. It took her a while to be convinced that she deserved it.

My mother was the sort of person who would go out of the way to help anyone else; that was just her nature. She spent most of her time doing things for other people. She didn't really give herself much time for herself, but she enjoyed doing what she did.

The funeral service in St James's Church, Hindpool, was a celebration of her life and I tried to incorporate her religious beliefs. And, to get across the Joan Grainger

Joan and her granddaughter Laura, the carnival mascot. (NW Evening Mail)

that people knew; as a family member, an old friend and as a public figure – all aspects. The hymns were Mam's favourites: 'The Lord is my Shepherd' and 'All things bright and beautiful,' – that was her outlook. We left the church to the Seekers playing 'The Carnival is Over' which we thought was appropriate; in lots of ways it covered Mam's life for all of us. It was also a song that when we lived in Australia, we would sing as we were driving along.

THREE

# VOICES FROM THE WORLD OF ENTERTAINMENT

## *Thomas Round*

*Thomas Round was born in Barrow in 1915. He had two brothers and a sister. He now lives at Bolton-le-Sands in Lancashire with his wife, Alice, to whom he has been married for sixty-nine years. He has been a joiner, a policeman and an RAF pilot. However, he is better known as an international opera singer, performing in grand opera, and as the lead tenor in many Gilbert & Sullivan operas, and in 'Gilbert & Sullivan for All' in leading theatres, concert halls, large auditoriums and small village and school halls, throughout the length and breadth of the British Isles. Thomas was interviewed on 7 September 2006.*

I was born at 32 Beech Street, Cemetery Cottages, Ormsgill, Barrow-in-Furness. I went to Hawcoat School which is now a private residence. [He also attended Holker Street School and Barrow Technical College.] The entrance to George Romney's home was about fifty or a hundred yards away and we as children used to walk up there and peer through the five-barred gate, scared out of our wits and ready to run off – never saw anybody that we knew but we knew that a famous painter lived there and we used to sneak through the gate of the house.

A lot of my youth was spent in Sowerby Woods; it was our playground, apart from the sand hills. We used to wander through those woods hour after hour, and it was a good picnic area. During the General Strike, they cut a lot of the trees down; they were allowed to dig out the roots for firewood for they were short of coal. They dried the tree roots for fuel for fires.

My family of six lived in a cottage in Beech Street, with three bedrooms and a little parlour which I used to think was lovely, but it was about eight feet square. I do now wonder how my family of six lived there – with difficulty I think, but I am amazed when I see the conversions they have done on those little cottages. Years ago, my father was the first to carry out improvements. He turned part of our back kitchen into a bathroom and built a wash-house in the back yard. (His father was also the first to have electricity installed in place of gas, and he re-roofed the cottage with Lakeland slate.)

My father had two allotments, one at the top of Beech Street, a wonderful vegetable garden with hens, and he had one further along on the top. Apart from vegetables, we had a pony (called Joey), and trap which we used to go about in. I remember a war memorial plaque at the end of Beech Street; my father was the instigator of that. I must go and see it, for someone told me it needs cleaning.

At first, the Cemetery Cottages Club was down at the bottom of Beech Street; it was a tin shack really and my father was the first secretary and treasurer of that until they moved into a new building further down the road, and I remember when I was serving my time as a joiner, my boss and I made the flag-pole for that and had it rigged up.

My father worked in the ironworks loading up the iron ore to be sent up the gantries to be dropped into the furnaces; that was a hard job. The conditions were poor with all the bending over; the sand and the slag and the iron ore running – stooping and sweating and drinking water; they got stomach cramps, so beer was supplied. They got a liking for it so it became a hard drinking community, although my father didn't drink.

My first job was as an apprentice joiner; there was a joiner's shop that did general repairs throughout the works and I served my time there, but I didn't finish my time. I remember one day working at my bench and at the next bench was my journeyman, one of the two I used to work with as an apprentice. He had a wonderful name – Amos Spry who came from Askam. I remember saying to him one day, 'When are you going to retire?' He said, 'When I drop dead at this bench.' I decided that was no good for me, so I decided to make other plans. (Thomas Round decided to leave his work as apprentice joiner and entered the Lancaster Borough Police Force in 1936 as PC 51.)

Singing first came into my life when I joined St Paul's Mission. They had a jolly good choir with a marvellous tenor line; my elder brother was a second tenor, my sister was contralto. I became involved because my future wife, Alice was a contralto and sang the contralto line, not that I knew the difference between any of those voices, I didn't. I used to be waiting in the vestry for the choir practice or the evening service to finish, so that Alice and I could continue our courting in the woods. Then, one evening I was asked to put the hymn books on the choir stalls which I did, and while I was in there, the choir stalls' door was locked, so I had to sit down where I was, so that was how I became a member of the choir.

My life became one round of music from the moment that I joined that choir when I was sixteen, and three weeks later I sang my first solo in a very breathy baritone voice. From then on, we formed our own concert party, the Merrymakers, and we sang at all the old people's homes and Alice and I did a double act, so from then on I started to sing quite a lot.

I appeared in a couple of amateur performances with the Lancaster Amateur and Dramatic Operatic Society with small parts before I went into the war at the end of 1941. After initial flying tests in this country, we were sent over to America and Canada; they started this Lend Lease – they couldn't possibly train pilots here because of the blackout and the bombing, so we went there; they were neutral so they hired private airfields. Originally we went over in civilian clothes because they were neutral so we couldn't go over in uniform. When I went, Pearl Harbour had already happened in December 1941, so we went over in uniform.

Thomas Round as a young tenor.
(*NW Evening Mail*)

After one or two extended leaves, I gave several concerts, including one at Barrow-in-Furness. [In 1944 the *North West Evening Mail* in Barrow wrote: 'MUSICAL TREAT AT BARROW. Much interest was aroused in the appearance of Flying Officer Thomas Round, a tenor of undoubted ability and with a bright future before him. Flying Officer Thomas Round was a joy to listen to. His interpretation and phrasing, backed by clearness of diction were very evident.']

I trained to fly in Terrell, Texas. I got my wings but then fortunately for me, I was at a house party and I was introduced to the adjutant of our airfield, a flight lieutenant, way above me – I was just a lowly flying boy and he was a wonderful pianist. He started playing the piano and he happened to play a song that I knew and I just got up and sang it, and from that moment on, it just started to roll on, because he played for me. We used to go all over the place singing in Dallas and elsewhere – all part of public relations.

When I was seconded into the American Air Force, I asked if I could be stationed as close to Dallas as possible, and they put me in an airfield about fifty miles away.

I used to sing and fly back to Dallas and broadcast a few times on the Pepsi School of Music. I was heard singing by the principal of the Hockaday School of Music, Ivan Dneprov, a very well known Russian tenor. I asked him if he would give me some lessons which he did and then he said he was planning to put on an opera called *Il Pagliacci* and asked if I would agree to play the principal role. I didn't know what grand opera was at that time and for me to play a vicious role like Canio was ridiculous. My voice would never do it, but I did it, and two years ago I recorded it for a programme *On with the Motley* – that great aria that Caruso and Gigli used to sing a lot. Gosh, I got away with it. I can still do it, but how I did it in those days as a young man with a few lessons behind me, I'll never know, but the reviews were very good and it made a lot of dollars for the American Red Cross and I said 'That's it, if I get out of this war alive, I'm going to try to become a professional singer,' so that started me off. They even gave me a letter of introduction to the principal of the Juilliard School of Music in New York, and I was offered a scholarship, but I was already married and I had a son I hadn't seen for two years, so I couldn't accept that anyway, but it was nice to have the offer.

A turning point in my music career was when I made my first encounter with the D'Oyly Carte Opera Company. I was stationed at Basingstoke, not far from London. The war had ended on the seventh of May, I think, so flying was haphazard then, so I travelled to London by tube to see a show. I saw a sign on the escalator, advertising the D'Oyly Carte Opera Company – Gilbert & Sullivan Operas. I had never heard of Gilbert & Sullivan or of the D'Oyly Carte Opera Company. They were playing at the King's Theatre Hammersmith – it was a Thursday and there was a matinée, so I thought well, I might as well go and see what it's all about. I asked a porter the way to Hammersmith.

The overture started which knocked me back in my seat, then when the curtain rose, on *The Mikado*, I couldn't believe what I was looking at – I'd never seen anything like that in my life. The costumes and the scenery, the music – absolutely fabulous. I mentally replaced the tenor singing the part of Nanki-Poo with myself.

In the interval I asked to see the manager and asked if I could audition. He told me to write to Mr Rupert D'Oyly Carte at the Savoy Hotel. I told him I wanted to sing there and then as I didn't know where I would be from one day to the next. My uniform won the day (I was a commissioned officer), so I sang for them after the show, between the matinée and evening performances. I was told to contact them as soon as I got out of the Air Force. When I was demobbed I returned to the Police Force and the DCC asked me if I was still interested and as I said I was, they sent me a score and script of *The Yeomen of the Guard*. They arranged for me to do a scene and offered me the contract right away. My life changed forever.

The Queen and Prince Philip came to a performance of *The Yeomen of the Guard* – the stage was built in the moat of the Tower of London and the seating was football stadium type of seating. That was the first time I was presented to Queen Elizabeth II – she was very nice. Then there was a command performance with the Sadler's Wells at the Coliseum and we did a section of *The Merry Widow*. [Thomas Round has toured many parts of the world with D'Oyly Carte and Sadler's Wells Opera Companies, appeared with Sir Thomas Beecham at the Festival Hall, starred

Thomas Round in the Lisdoonie Hotel, Barrow, 2006, following his interview. He was then aged ninety-one years and was still going strong. He was in fine voice and sang a few bars of 'Take a pair of sparkling eyes'. *(Alice Leach)*

in the BBC production of *La Traviata* and starred in the film of the story of Gilbert & Sullivan, been on the same bill as Norman Wisdom and played *The Mikado* on Broadway where he was called the 'Gilbert and Sullivan Sinatra'. However, he has never forgotten his roots and always seeks to promote his home town, Furness and the nearby English Lake District.]

I was invited to be President of the Savoyards many years ago and I have once again been asked. I have been coming here over the years singing as a professional, doing concerts in the former Public Hall and the Forum in Barrow and in Ulverston. In September 1981 'Gilbert and Sullivan for All' returned to Barrow and I performed with Donald Adams and the Savoyards at Barrow Civic Hall. In 1991 I starred in a Gilbert and Sullivan Festival at the Swan Hotel, Newby Bridge. I shall never forget our weekends in the Lake District.

Looking back, I have had a wonderful life in my chosen career and have met countless numbers of marvellous people. Once again, Gilbert provides the perfect ending [from Thomas Round's autobiography, *A Wand'ring Minstrel, I*]:

> Spring and Summer pleasure you
> Autumn, aye, and Winter too.
> Every season has its cheer
> Life is lovely all the year.

# David Marcus

*Born David Clay in Bradford in 1949, David Marcus has lived and worked in Barrow for over thirty years as a theatre director and drama coach. He has designed costumes and sets for Barrow and Walney Amateurs and has worked extensively with children's drama groups in Furness schools. In 1973 he was instrumental in the formation of the Savoyards and in association with them, has directed and played lead parts in many Gilbert and Sullivan shows. Arguably the Furness Mystery Plays of 1988 were David Marcus's most successful productions. David was interviewed on 6 June 2006.*

I always knew what Mystery Plays were. They were initially done by the clergy inside the churches to teach the Bible stories to an illiterate populace; they got too big for the churches and they were taken outside into the churchyards, and then the tradesmen thought that they could advertise their craft, so they got involved. The carpenters might do the Noah's Ark story because they could build the boat, the tailor might do the Three Kings, so they could show off their beautiful fabrics and exquisite needlework. The churches didn't like this advertising to tell the Bible stories, so the tradesmen were pushed into the streets – hence the pageant wagons. Each play travelled round the town or city, and there are many cycles of Mystery Plays: York, Coventry, Chester and Wakefield.

When I was approached by English Heritage to present Mystery Plays in Furness Abbey, I read all the cycles and I picked what I thought was the best of each, and what I thought was manageable. I took away the medievalisms but kept in the alliterations. I hope I made them more understandable to a modern audience. I decided to use the whole of the abbey and to promenade the plays; for instance, to put God on top of the tower and the Crucifixion behind the altar through the window, and to use the stream for the baptism. I wish I'd known then what I know now, for logistically speaking, it was a nightmare to do. Then we had the Royal Visit of Prince Edward and we had frogmen in the stream looking for devices. It was, however, fantastic to look back on, and so many people were involved. I loved the music for it; it was all computerised really by Stephanie Soby Jones. I had ideas in mind and we had lots of discussions at her house and burned the midnight oil.

David Marcus in the abbey grounds during rehearsals. *(NW Evening Mail)*

David Marcus with Peter Duncan, former *Blue Peter* presenter, who played Christ. *(NW Evening Mail)*

David Marcus with Prince Edward, opening night. *(NW Evening Mail)*

Furness Abbey, 1127–1537. (Roy Chatfield)

I remember the Temple Play as being dramatic. I wanted the audience to participate within it and they walked through the temple before they witnessed the scene and they had the sellers and the belly dancers there first hand, trying to barter with them. We also used the audience as the Red Sea and we parted them. When we had the trial scene I had the cast interspersed with the audience, shouting 'Crucify Him!' 'Crucify Him!' One or two of them were thumped by members of the audience. The actual Crucifixion was made more poignant on the night of the storm. A mist descended, adding another dimension to the lighting. It all became so real, and when I joined them in the nave of the abbey church, my cast knelt and some of the audience knelt with them.

I always look back on the 1988 Furness Mystery Plays with great fondness and pride because it brought a lot of people together and I made a lot of friends through them. I remember being in the Abbey Tavern about one o'clock in the morning and they were just putting the finishing touches to the lighting and they said, 'Would you come and pull the switch and put the lights on?' That was the first time Furness Abbey had ever been lit by electricity in its history and I was very moved and privileged to be doing the 'switch on'.

I've done Mystery Plays, I've done Shakespeare, I've played Thomas Becket in *Murder in the Cathedral*. But, I'm best known for doing Dame in pantomime.

David Marcus as
Mother Goose, 2004.
*(NW Evening Mail)*

*From 1994 to 2006 David Marcus produced eleven highly successful pantomimes, playing
the Dame for Pumpkin Productions in Forum 28.*

I look back at every show I've done and ask myself why did I do that like I did, and
think, I'd like to do that again, I'd do it better, but I think that's a natural
progression that's part of the learning process because I always maintain that the day
you stop learning is the day you give up.

I regard Barrow as my home and I would do anything within reason as long as it's
legal, so for the future I still see myself directing shows, still producing – I hope so
anyway. Sometimes it can be very frustrating. It's a job you've got to love, otherwise
you wouldn't do it. I do love it and I'm happy to continue. I'm very lucky to be
involved in work that I love doing, so I'm very fortunate.

## Danny Patterson

*Danny Patterson was born in 1931 in Barrow. He has become one of the town's best loved singers and entertainers, playing clubs and pubs as well as compèring and singing for many charitable fund-raising events. Danny was interviewed on 14 June 2006.*

The Flamingos were Johnny Chapman, the leader; Larry Johnson, the pianist; Brian Parkinson, the guitarist; Tony Gregory, the string bassoonist; Jack Smith, the drummer; and myself. We once got a gig in Oman in the '60s. A telex came through to Vickers and we thought it was a joke; it was an oil company. We played till five in the morning and sat on the veranda watching the sun come up. Two days later we were back in the shipyard working on a submarine. The Flamingos lasted many years – basically the group is still going. We play in a jazz club in the Conservative Club in Barrow every other week. Syd Patterson plays piano and trumpet. He's in his eighties and used to play in the London Palladium Orchestra.

   I love singers like Vic Damone and Neil Diamond, but Sinatra was the governor, no question about that. I saw him in Las Vegas. He was seventy-four, and I thought if he has a heart attack I'm on that stage, because I know every song he's going to sing. There was only one Sinatra.

The 'Flamingos' with Danny Patterson. 'One of your Sunday Attractions' at the King's Arms Hotel. *(Danny Patterson)*

During a concert in July 2007, Trad Jazz trumpeter Les Bull teamed up with Danny to give a moving rendition of the old Frank Sinatra favourite, 'You Make Me Feel So Young'. Mr Bull paid tribute to Danny – 'Danny's been a legend in Barrow for a long time. I regard him as chairman of the board.' (NW Evening Mail)

My daughter, Yvonne, is a well-known singer. There was always music playing in the house and she was quick at learning a song, and she formed a little band of her own. She has sung all over the world, eventually working on the cruise liners. I went a few times on the cruise liners and sang with the band. I still sing in Yvonne's shows.

I pick the jobs I want to do now. During a musical career, you grow up with your contemporaries and you tend to get the same audiences all the way through. I've had a wonderful life.

*Danny Patterson died in 2007.*

FOUR

# VOICES FROM THE WORLD OF INDUSTRY

## *Benjamin High*

*Benjamin (Ben) High was born in Millom in Cumbria in 1920. He attended Lapstone Road Infant School and later won a scholarship to Millom Grammar School. Benjamin was interviewed by his daughter, Vanessa Allen, in 2005.*

My scholarship at Millom Grammar School only lasted four years, so I joined the shipyard in 1936 at the age of fifteen. Apart from an occasional visit to Barrow from Millom, I didn't know Barrow very well and I'd never been across the High Level Bridge before, until my interview.

My wages as an apprentice were 7s 1d a week, but it cost me 5s a week train fare. When I was sixteen I started to pay National Insurance, so my wages went down to 5s 11d a week. The train fare went up to 5s 3d a week and my mother used to give me a shilling pocket money. I would buy a couple of cowboy books from Millom market for 7d. We worked from half-past seven in the morning until 5 o'clock at night and every Saturday morning. It was a forty-seven hour week. As an apprentice, I had night school three nights a week. After work I used to make my way to Church Street to get freshened up at the public washrooms. I then went on to Melville's Fish and Chip Shop in Dalton Road.

To become an apprentice I had to sit an exam and the top four, including me, opted for being electricians. The electrical trade was in its infancy at that time. When they wanted some plans tracing for the Coffee House wiring, before it opened, I did that in the office. At that time, the electrical department on the engineering side was responsible for the welding department. The electrical apprentices were invited to have a spell on welding, which I did in 1937. I was on it for fourteen months and then, when the Second World War started, we were all recalled to do electrical work on the conversion of trawlers to mine sweepers. After that we were transferred to work on the guns in the ordnance department.

The first work I did as an apprentice was on the *Awatea*, a boat used on the Australia/New Zealand run. In fact, there's a photograph of the *Awatea* in the Investigative Clinic corridor at Furness General Hospital. The journeyman I was working for was called Tommy Hetherington and he was a real gentleman. What a role model he was! He would give me a shilling a week himself to help me out.

From a sheltered existence at the grammar school, it was a big shock to the system, working in the boiler room, cabins and the engine room. In August 1936, I moved up to the Motor Man's Corner, behind St Patrick's Road. We were building welding generating sets: two forty-horsepower motors, linked with a coupling, mounted on channel bars, which had to be ordered from the boiler shop. Over the coupling a framework was made, which had to be ordered from the engine smithy. It was my job to go and order these parts. It was good experience.

Life was hard in those days for the working classes. At Barrow Island Junction, the night shift would be making their way back to the train and the children would be there, waiting to ask whether the men had any bread left. On Fridays, after the shift finished, an artist used to place his board on the pavement on the corner, near St Patrick's Church. The lads would give any spare change they had. The picture I remember most was of a loaf of bread with the words 'Easy to cut, but hard to get'.

'Have you any bread?' *(Jo Rose from* Our Barrow – Barrow Island, *by Alice Leach, 1981)*

Many men used to stand outside the work gates 'on the market', and if any work was available, the trade foreman would go to the gate and say 'You, you and you'. The others went home. *(Jo Rose from* Our Barrow – Barrow Island, *by Alice Leach, 1981)*

*Ben was about to finish his electric apprenticeship when he was sent to Plymouth to work to convert a forward turret from the* Belfast. *After wrestling with forty-three core lead-covered cables to get them into the junction box, he decided to go back to welding proper in 1941.*

After the war I was on the engineering side and we built all the equipment for the ships: the evaporators, the condensers, gear boxes. We were also employed building machinery, particularly cement machinery. Vickers had a cement division and we did jobs all over the world. We also had a chemical division based in Southampton. The chemical division teamed up with Zimmer in Germany to do work in the Soviet Union – the first time in 1962 and the second being 1964. I worked down in the Ukraine in a place called Severodonetsk; it was really a pioneer town full of young vibrant Russians. First time I went, there were 40,000 there and on my second visit, two years later, it had grown to 60,000 – very interesting. They were all eager to learn about us as I was about them. English was their second language. I learnt all sorts of phrases, particularly about how to order meals and also to get round Moscow. I'd gone there with the intention of enjoying the experience. I wasn't looking over my shoulder for security men or anything like that. It was very good. In 1961 I went to Israel to work on a cement plant; a repair job was necessary from work which Vickers had installed in about 1955. I've had a very varied career. I've also worked up at the Tyne and down at Coventry.

I enjoyed my working life in Vickers and found it very rewarding because we had an exceptionally good management on the engineering side. Vickers' engineers nowadays doesn't get much of a mention; it's all the shipyard. But there was so much work going on in the engineering department, so diverse and interesting. People we met were great. I enjoyed every minute of it, mainly because of the people I worked with. Conditions were hard but it was the fellowship of your workmates and their sense of humour that made the job worthwhile.

The whole business now – asbestos, we were exposed to that terribly. In the welding department, we were using electrodes, and the fumes were highly particulate, and this was necessary because of the change of product for all the steels that were changing, and the subsequent treatment of them the pre-heating – that was necessary. Then everything improved except for the equipment. We still had the same helmet, the same gloves and that was all – nothing changed. Fume extraction wasn't even considered as a necessity by the management. You had to improvise and make your own, using the compressed air and adapting different bits of piping to pull the fumes away from you. It was a bit backward.

*Ben retired from Vickers in 1982. He shared a happy retirement with his wife until her death in 1997, and with his friends, participating in outdoor pursuits and other interests.*

I have a very good friend, Len Flay, who comes to see me every week and he's eighty-six. He was a shop steward and we have a great relationship. We used to go fell walking together, cycling, camping and he's still doing it. He comes to see me on his push-bike from North Scale. [Len Flay died in December 2006.]

A retirement presentation being made by John Barker, manager of the north-west shop to George McLaughlin, head foreman, taken in the north-west shop, *c.* 1980. Left to right: Bill Smith, John Barker, Huey Rae, George Mclaughlin, and Ben High, Head foreman welder. *(Vickers' Press by kind permission of John Barker)*

I was one of the first casualties of the Legionnaire's disease in 2002. I've lost many of the things that made life worthwhile, and I no longer go for walks; I can no longer sing in the choirs. I am a life member of the Male Voice Choir and a founder member of the Furness Chorale and I can no longer participate in those things. I'd very much like to. I spent over ten weeks in hospital, both in Furness General and in Ulverston Hospital.

*Ben died in February 2007. He is survived by a son and three daughters.*

# Katie Percy

*Katie Percy was born in 1920 in Barrow and was educated at primary and secondary schools on Walney Island. She was one of six children. She married in 1941 and has four children. Katie Percy now lives in Southampton and her story is a written account.*

I was almost nineteen years old when the Second World War broke out in September 1939. In 1941, women without children were required to register for war work at the local Department of Labour. Barrow was an industrial town with a large shipbuilding firm [Vickers Armstrong] and a steelworks.

I was called up in March 1941 and directed to Barrow Steelworks, as were many other girls of my age. Most of the girls were very disappointed as they had hoped to be sent to Vickers. The steelworks was a truly dreadful place to work in! Talk about 'Dante's inferno!' Heat, dust, bits of discarded metal lying about the red-stained floor made it a real hazard to walk about in! We had to be constantly looking down to make sure we didn't trip over them. Our skin became stained red from the iron-ore floating about in the murky air as were our boiler-suits, and turbans which we wore to protect our hair.

We all sat operating the rollers set in the floor. At the far end was the Siemens furnace, and when it opened, a blast of white-hot heat travelled the entire length of the mill. The furnace men, stripped to the waist, grappled the huge glowing ingot to get it on to the first set of rollers which were operated by a man in the crane above which sent it to the first huge press, showering white-hot sparks which danced like fireflies in the gloom.

The press squeezed it as effortlessly as though it were a lump of butter, so that it came out the other side smaller and narrower, and dropped it on to the next set of rollers.

Now it was our turn to operate our levers and send the hot monster slithering along the rollers to the next pressing to be operated by the two girls in the next section. After it

Katie Percy photographed on Walney Island by her brother, William, in 1937. *(William Percy)*

passed, the sweat rolled off us, and we had to struggle into our coats, to avoid getting a chill. The Rolling Mill was beside Walney Channel from where chill winds swept through the gaps in the corrugated iron walls of the old Victorian building.

This whole operation was repeated the entire length of the mill, until it became a steel railway line. The last operator worked the billet shears, which trimmed off the jagged edges and then sent it rattling away to the railway trucks outside.

All the girls hated the job, which was dirty and dangerous. We sat just feet from where the ingot dropped out of the press and rumbled along the rollers; it coiled up like an attacking snake and shot towards the hapless operators. Our only protection was a low metal fence. We had to leap out and flee from the danger.

The girls grumbled constantly about the hazards and the two shifts we had to work, especially the late afternoon one. We finished at eleven o'clock in the evening and had to struggle home in the blackout with the ever-present fear that the air raid siren might blare out, and the air raid wardens would direct us to the shelters. As well as all this, the wages were miserly compared to those that girls in Vickers were earning.

We were all so dissatisfied I decided to write a letter to the manager. This was ignored. One day, a few weeks later, we all decided on some drastic action. At tea break I locked the canteen door and we all sat there waiting the result, for another ingot was due to come out of the furnace and couldn't be rolled without our presence. We didn't have long to wait. A huge banging on the door and shouting from the mill foreman made us shout. 'We're on strike!' With that they sent for the manager who arrived and was furious, banging on the door like the others.

Part of the blast furnace plant of the Barrow Haematite Steel Co. Ltd. *(Published with permission of Barrow Borough Council)*

Brady's wagon at the entrance to the steelworks, when full-scale work was in production at the steelworks. T. Brady & Sons were the major haulage contractors to Barrow Steel, later to become British Steel Corporation. (R. Brady, Managing Director of T. Brady & Son)

However, he promised to see us at three o'clock providing we went back to the mill and got the steel rolling again. I was the only one who dared go to his office and listen to the tirade that followed. At the end of it, he calmed down and said we would be receiving ten shillings a week rise. The sum we were paid was what boys under eighteen earned before they were called up. I was triumphant and it showed. He asked me if it was I who had written the letter and I said 'Yes, but we were all in agreement.' He then asked my name and wrote something down. The following week I was sacked.

Straight away I went to the Labour Exchange to apply for another job, but they refused to give me a job telling me they'd had a call from the steelworks saying I'd been sacked for being a troublemaker. I tramped the town and finally found a job on the LMS Railway. Barrow had been bombed and the station ticket office and refreshment rooms reduced to a pile of rubble. I worked alongside another girl with a gang of bricklayers. We had to sit astride a trestle cleaning bricks for the 'brickies' to rebuild the parts the Luftwaffe had smashed.

It was a mind-blowing job, rough on the hands, and tough on the arms, and did nothing to endear me to Hitler. But, I was to get my own back on him later in the war. I had to leave my LMS job in 1942 because I was having my first child. My husband was employed as a farm worker on poor wages, and I missed my wages very much. It was imperative that I began work again. When my son was fourteen months old, my neighbour, whose husband was in the RAF, offered to mind my child as she was at home with two young sons.

I immediately applied for work at Vickers and was offered a job as a milling machine operator making bomb-door brackets and pivot bolts for Wellington bombers. At last I was getting my revenge on Hitler for having to clean all those bricks his Luftwaffe bombers had knocked out of Barrow's station. Compared to working in the steelworks, it was a treat operating a milling machine. Other girls worked on lathes.

The work was clean and far better paid than that at the steelworks. An experienced engineer came around and supervised our work, testing the pieces of duralumin with a micrometer as it was important for them to be accurate. We had to turn out a certain number of items, but milling more than this earned us a bonus on top of our wages.

Some girls worked shifts, but I began work on the second buzzer at half-past seven in the morning until the lunch hour at midday. I then rushed home to eat a sandwich of bread and cheese – if I was lucky – and scoured the shops for items of food to make up our meagre rations, then back to work again at one o'clock till half-past five. Sometimes it was compulsory to work overtime until seven o'clock; it was very tiring and we were always hungry, sometimes only having boiled potatoes for dinner. Barrow seemed to be always short of food. Friends who visited Blackpool and Morecambe were astonished at the amount of food obtainable there. Barrow, it seemed, was cut off from a lot of deliveries because it was a peninsula, isolated by Morecambe Bay.

There were many worthy women who kept the shipyard and steelworks going and producing the weapons needed to defeat Hitler.

The entrance to the steelworks, saved by the foresight of the Brady Haulage Firm when the Barrow Haematite Steel Company closed in 1983. The arch was dismantled brick by brick and re-erected in Brady's Yard. The wagon on the right of the arch was bright red with the initials T.B. for the founder, Tom Brady. On the left of the arch are curtain-sided trailers, above which can be seen part of Barrow cemetery. (Bob Herbert, c. 1989)

## James Dunn

*James (Jim) Dunn was born in Barrow in 1945. He has one brother and four sisters. He is married to Ann and has two daughters. He was educated at St Mary's and St Aloysius's RC Schools in Barrow. He has served his time as an apprentice shipwright, been a shipwright lofting instructor and a college lecturer. Having obtained the necessary qualifications, he entered the teaching profession, teaching at Alfred Barrow Comprehensive School until his retirement in July 2007. Jim was interviewed on 3 November 2006.*

I left school at the age of fifteen years and in 1961, I began a five-year apprenticeship; my idea of becoming an apprentice shipwright stemmed from the days when I used to watch a relative of mine working on his boat down the channel side and I was always amazed at the way he could use the wood-working tools, and when he told me he did this as a full-time job at the shipyard, as a shipwright,

Back row, left to right: Albert Cowan, labourer; Jack Brewer, shipwright; Ernie Corbett, labourer; Joe Darragh, shipwright; Jack Sergeant, shipwright; Alan Newsham, shipwright; Norman Whinnerah, labourer. Middle row: Dick Pratt, labourer; Ned Beach, shipwright; Sammy Rutter, labourer. Front row: 'Pom' Woodburn, labourer; Bert Jevons, shipwright; Eric Threlfall, labourer; Arthur Gill, shipwright; Hector Burston, shipwright. *(Alice Leach)*

I thought that was the job for me, and it was the only job I ever wanted to do. Little did I know when I went into the shipyard there were two types of shipwrights: an iron working shipwright and a wood working shipwright, and after spending four months in the training school, which was Hunter's Yard in those days, I was sent out into the top yard – the shipyard, and the first job they gave me was working in iron work, which was a big, rough, heavy, dirty, dusty job, and after about two months of this, I went to the head foreman and I said 'This isn't the job for me, it wasn't what I thought.' The head foreman at that time was a guy called John Preece, and he asked me what I wanted and I explained that I thought I would be working in wood, but he told me I would have to work in iron as well. He was really a progressive foreman because he thought that people worked better if they were happy, so he took me over to the spar shed where the launch squad worked and he said 'This is the wood working area, would you like to work in here?' and as I said 'Yes', he told me I could start working there immediately. That was how I came to be working in the spar shed with Ned Beach, Hector Burston, Arthur Gill, Ray White – some fantastic men.

The first job they gave us was down on the berth ramming slivers underneath the cradle; the cradle was the structure that supports the ship as it sits on top of the slideways. The first day there struck me as being strange – the whole squad were very big, very tough men; there was Alan Newsham about six foot five, a giant of a man. I was working with Ned Beach and the job he gave me was to drive in wedges – big, long slivers as they were called – into the cradle to push the cradle against the ship. I can remember Ned giving me a rollicking because I wasn't taking enough care working with timber, so he showed me how to do it. Because I was keen on rugby, and Ned was a keen rugby man, as were all the squad, and as Ned was one of the leading lights on the launching squad, we became mates and so it was quite easy to make friends with all the other shipwrights and I thoroughly enjoyed the experience.

I worked in the graving dock with your dad [Alice Leach's dad, Ned Beach] and one job was docking HMS *Mohawk*. [HMS *Mohawk* was ship no. 1063 and was launched 5 April 1962 by Mrs J.M. Villiers for the Royal Navy.]

The hull beneath the waterline needed cleaning in the graving dock, which is still there today although it is not in use as a graving dock. Ned Beach and all the launching squad used to bring the ship in – open the dock gates and float the ship in, close the dock gates and pump all the water out. And as they were pumping the water out, the shipwrights, the launch-way squad, used to stand on the steps, called altars, at the side of the dock, and as the ship lowered down, they dropped breast shores into place, so when the ship actually settled on the blocks, it was supported both sides by the shores, to stop any distortion of the shell plating.

Our job was to make sure that they landed directly on frames inside the ship and as we let the water out, the ship slowly landed on the keel blocks. It was the shipwright's job to make sure that the fore end and the aft end were perfectly in line with the centre line of the docks; after that, of course, we could start to place bilge blocks that support the bilges of the ship. That describes to some extent, my experience of working in the graving dock.

Some of those men I had been working with on the berth were reaching retiring age and in winter months it could be bitterly cold, so on retiring age, they used to be sent to the 'mock-up' where I worked, even when I was an apprentice. A 'mock-up' is a full-scale model made out of wood before it goes into production. One of the funniest things I remember was one day when we were sitting and talking, somebody just happened to mention Willie Horne (a household name to the people of Barrow), and they all stood up and took their caps off. I was sitting there with my beret on and Ned belted me over the head with his cap and said, 'Stand up and take your hat off when we mention Willie.' I thought the camaraderie was fantastic, to join in, talking about rugby and the great legends of rugby, like Willie Horne, Jimmy Lewthwaite, Jack Grundy and Frank Castle.

I was there until I had served my apprenticeship and then I went into the mould loft which is where they draw the shape of the ship out on the floor for other shipwrights to make moulds (patterns). Platers draw round it and then we had to make a mocking and the platers then bend or roll it around this particular mocking. Going into the loft gave me an interest in geometry, trigonometry and maths, and I have been interested in maths ever since; it was useful to me because the stuff that I did as an apprentice gave me an impetus for going on for further qualifications, so I owe quite a lot to the shipwright department.

The *Invincible* was launched by HM Queen Elizabeth II on 3 May 1977. The ship took part in the Falklands War. *(NW Evening Mail)*

Jim Dunn in his office at Alfred Barrow School. *(G. Garvey)*

In 1974, I went into the training department as a shipwright lofting instructor. During that time I was a part-time teacher at Furness College teaching Technical Drawing, Maths and Physics. In 1984 I left the shipyard to become a lecturer at Furness College. The next stage in my career was to obtain qualifications to work in mainstream education. After obtaining a Bachelor of Education degree and a Diploma in Advanced Education Studies, I went as a supply teacher in local primary and secondary schools, and finally I was successful in gaining a post at Alfred Barrow Comprehensive School in Barrow where I am still employed.

I teach Maths and Physics; the whole job of shipbuilding revolved round maths and physics. Physics is an important subject; it doesn't just happen in laboratories, it's all around you, certainly in shipbuilding – all engineering and far out in space. You'll find physics everywhere. Maths and physics complement each other.

When I have some respite from duties as a teacher and as a magistrate, I enjoy writing poetry. I first became interested in poetry when I was at Secondary School (St Aloysius). I used to love English at school – the written word. I find that by writing poetry you can express yourself, but it does require sitting down and searching for the right word to get the message across. I always remember when you [Alice Leach] once gave us a poem to review for homework and I said, 'It doesn't rhyme Miss,' and you replied, 'It's what you feel.' [Jim was taught English for a short time by Alice Leach.]

## *A Breed Apart by James F. Dunn*

A Barrow lad's just mongrel stock, forebears from other lands,
Hired to work this barren waste with other foreign gangs,
There's no such thing as a Barrow lad, he has no pedigree,
He might speak about his great granddad, but then he's from Inisfree.

His great grandma, she's not from here, she hails from a Cornish town,
Her dad, he came to work your shafts, where the rich, red ore was found.
No, a Barrow lad's a mongrel, not from pure bred lines,
but brought here to do the job, in your treacherous iron mines.

So, a Barrow lad's a mongrel without a pedigree?
Well, take a look around this town and tell me what you see,
Compare this town to anywhere, wherever in the land.
These Barrow men in one hundred years had formed a solid band.

These skilled and granite artisans entirely on their own,
Carved out this jewel in the north and worked it stone by stone.
Through famine and disease they toiled and two world wars they gave;
A son, a dad, a brother, their finest and their brave.

Listen to a Barrow lad boast of his abbey's vaulted trees,
Let him tell of God's own country surrounded by the seas,
Pause and let him fondly muse of Lakeland fells beyond,
Where Wordsworth, Coleridge with Southey roamed and formed a fraternal bond.

Feel for him as he speaks with pride about historic Piel,
About their gallant lifeboat crew those hardened men of steel,
Called only when there's danger from tempest, storm or tide,
And count the many lives they've saved and valiant friends who died.

Those shipyard men and ships they've built, craftsmen of world renown,
The skills passed down are the skills that made this little Barrow town.
You spoke of ore, what cost of life, that nugget began it all,
From majestic town hall, seen for miles, to gigantic Dev. Dock Hall.

Beware, take care, don't ridicule, before you know those people.
Those diamond folk who built our town, in the shade of Hindpool's steeple.
Don't dare to call them mongrel, they care not where you're from,
For every inch of this great town was built by its own son.

They've just earned their pedigree
They've earned it with their blood
They're proud to be a Barrow lad,
And bloody well they should.

'Spirit of Barrow' by Christopher Kelly, sculptor. The statues of the workers are: a welder (for skills), a fitter (for courage), a riveter (for labour) and a female electrician (for progress).

Christopher Kelly's other public commissions for the Borough of Barrow-in-Furness are Willy Horne – Rugby League Captain of Barrow, England & Great Britain (2004) and Emlyn Hughes – Captain of Liverpool and England (2007).

# FIVE

# CONSERVATIONISTS' VOICES

## David Gill

*David Gill was born in Dalton in 1961. He was educated at schools in Furness. From a very early age it was evident that he had a very special gift with animals – and a passion! On leaving Victoria High School, he attended Myerscough Agricultural College, Lancashire, and his first job was as an animal nutritionist. It was while working as Regional Manager for the north of England, for Roche vitamin and mineral products that an idea came to him that would change his life forever. David was interviewed on 19 March 2007.*

I had a fantastic job. I went on farms every day trying to resolve problems with cattle and sheep. I loved it. Then one day, in 1993, I had what was like a Damascus Road experience (without religion). 'I had a desire to bring conservation to the public, to create a place like no other, where the visitor, through a unique close-up wild encounter could form a bond with nature, a place that would facilitate world-wide conservation' (extract from the Guide Book).

### Getting started

I had quite a large collection of animals before I built the South Lakes Wild Animal Park in Dalton-in-Furness, Cumbria, because what I ended up doing was getting involved with rescuing animals from the RSPCA. When they had no homes for them I used to take them on, so I ended up with a house full of racoons, coatis, wallabies, parrots, pheasants, doves and ponies. That was at the back of my house at Romney Avenue, and I had two acres of ground with that house. I just had an amazing collection and that's where it developed, and then we moved into here. I brought all those animals here, and then Chester Zoo helped me a little bit and they brought me some guanacos, which are like lambs or llamas, and one or two antelope species. But it was very basic when I first started, with rabbits, guinea pigs, a few wallabies, parrots – it was very simple.

From that simple beginning I am now totally committed to working around the world, protecting endangered species and habitats. At the zoo we don't just talk about conservation, we do it! I get frustrated about the amount of people who love

A poster at the zoo. *(Alice Leach)*

to have meetings and just talk because by the time everybody has discussed it and come up with an idea, everything's gone: the forest has gone, it's all been cut down, so it's too late. My concept was that you can't just talk about it, you've got to do it; to go out and get your hands dirty, and be active and to break the mould of main zoos, which was just to pay lip service. Many zoos' ideas of conservation are to tell people about forest destruction, about the trading in animal parts, but my idea is not just to tell them, but to get out there and make a difference by stopping the forest destruction and the trade in animals and to play a very direct, influential role for changing small and large parts of the planet. In Sumatra, in particular, we look after and protect a forest that is bigger than Cumbria. I'm therefore a big believer in not just talking but getting out there and doing it.

After two years of doing this park, I became aware, all of a sudden, out of nowhere, that tigers were actually on the verge of extinction and nobody was doing anything at all for these tigers in Sumatra. There was purported to be around 450–500 left, but the government was saying, if nothing is done, within five years they'll all be gone. It was then that I realised I had to take some very direct action; initially I just got involved and I started raising money, but then I realised I had to be an official charity to do it properly, so we set this up, and it is an official fact that we are the biggest fundraisers for Sumatran Tigers' Conservation in the world, because virtually nobody else is doing it.

We work in three very big areas of Sumatra, protecting areas of forest, and our teams are the best tiger people in the world. I'm very proud of the work we've done over there, because today there is still probably around 350 to 400 tigers, so they haven't gone, and we are ten to eleven years on from when we started, so I think what we have done has had a very significant effect, especially with the government out there. Sadly, the forest is still disappearing as fast as ever, and it's not going to stop either. The volume of wood that's cut down in Sumatra every day is beyond belief, so it has only got a few years left and it's all going to be gone. They are replanting areas but with eucalyptus and acacia which is totally unnatural to Sumatra and nothing lives in it. It might as well be a desert for a tiger or for a monkey, because they can't live there. It's a sad scenario and I just felt somebody had to help because the Indonesian people are very conscious that there are four types of tiger left and four types of tiger have become extinct, and two of those types that are extinct were in Indonesia – the Bali tiger and the Java tiger. They are all extinct, and the last one was the Sumatran, and they were watching it disappear, so it was quite an embarrassment for them to have this going on, so they were very welcoming to us to help them. We have a very high level partnership with the Indonesian government. Because the situation has been highlighted and because of the internet, we have sponsors from all over the world: China, America, Australia – you name it. [1996 was 'The year of the tiger' at South Lakes Wild Animal Park when the first tigers arrived. Today there are four tigers in the park.]

A photograph of one of the tigers taken at the zoo. (Alice Leach)

Today there are over seventy different species of animals in the park, as confirmed by my daughter, Amy, who is the registrar. My favourite animal is a rhino; there's something quite special about rhinos, they are one of the most misunderstood animals. Everybody knows that tigers are stealthy, amazingly powerful and special. A tiger is a solo killer, and just a special cat, way more special than lions, because they do hunt on their own and it takes skill, but the rhino is often seen as a vicious, nasty, charging horrible animal, and it's not. They are just really laid back, gentle giants, like dinosaurs; they've really not changed over millions of years. They are like a whale in some respects, because they have this tiny eye and a great big head; that eye tells you everything about what the animal is thinking. As soon as the rhinos see me, these three-ton animals come and line up and put their tails up for a tickle. They are fantastically gentle. They just eat grass, they have a horn to protect themselves from other rhinos, it's not to hurt people – they are just so loving. The biggest trauma in my life was when I had to shoot one of our rhinos that had had a very bad accident.

David Gill with his favourite animals. (*NW Evening Mail*)

That was the most dramatically upsetting thing that has ever happened to me in my whole life, and it took me a lot of years to even mention it. The challenge for me then was to replace that animal in the world, so I made sure I got a breeding programme set up. At this moment two female rhinos are pregnant.

## Caring for the animals

A successful specialist breeding programme is essential and you have to be part of a big team. There's got to be a lot of facilities available, a lot of expertise, so therefore, we're part of a worldwide organisation. We are members of the European Association of Zoos which organises breeding programmes for Europe and each programme for each species has a co-ordinator. It's all voluntary. I think there are nine different international programmes for different species. We manage them, and it's all done very technically on a computer, where every single animal, its history, its parents, its grandparents, even where it was caught in the wild from all those years ago; all that history is in computers.

All the details are there and we then bring animals together by computer dating – genetic rather than by looks. We look at the genetics and we say that these two are unrelated, and bring them together. For instance, only this week [March 2007] we had one Emperor Tamarind that came in from the Czech Republic, and one from Denmark, and they've been brought to us to make a new pair, which is totally unrelated. So the animals come from all over to be paired up like this, and it's very important that that happens, because traditionally in zoos, people just bought and sold animals, and very often a zoo would have a brother and sister pair, breed and produce a brother and sister pair, and then they would get sold to somebody else, who would keep them as a brother and sister pair, and you would get terrible inbreeding problems. It's very important that we manage species very well, and so all our animals are part of these programmes, so when it's necessary to move them, we move them. It's often very upsetting; two of our giraffes have to move very soon, one to Belfast, and one to Cork, and we're very upset, because we've grown those giraffes up from being very small to very big, and now they've got to go to be breeding mares.

Medical care is very important. We don't have a full-time vet but we do have a vet who's worked with us for nearly thirteen years, since I started. He's from Broughton, and he's become very adapted to looking after the animals here, and we work together. We built a new veterinary centre last year, so now we can do all our own operations here. Medical veterinary care is very important, but the wonderful thing about technology is that you're never on your own. You're only an e-mail or a phone call away from experts around the world, who are so happy to help you with any problem you've got. If, for instance, you don't know anything about something like a Condor, you could e-mail immediately and get an answer the next day to your problem.

When it comes to providing food for the different species of animals, we don't seem to have any problems. There's a lot of legislation now with food; for instance, with meat and meat by-products. We have to register everything in and out – every

David Gill with a giraffe at the zoo. *(NW Evening Mail)*

bone has to be picked up and actually taken back and rendered and weighed, and logged. It's unbelievable the rules to do with meat feeding nowadays. We have had problems sometimes getting meat, for instance in the foot and mouth epidemic, and with the BSE situation where all animals that had died had to be rendered, and so therefore getting animals in was very difficult. We have amazing support from ASDA, Marks & Spencer and Kwik Save in Barrow. ASDA and M&S in particular have been involved with us now for about twelve years and we go every day, and all their waste, as they put it, is perfect stuff, and comes to us every day from there. Without them the animals wouldn't get the variety; they would just get a set diet every day because we'd have to buy it all in, but because they give us all this tremendous variety, the animals do get amazingly good food, and we're very grateful to these retailers. I know they are very happy to do it because it saves them landfill problems and we're all recycling. The animals get a great benefit.

Animals can't tell us if they have got a tummy ache or a headache, so my totally committed staff who work outside, and who share my passion for animals have to be extremely alert and astute. The animals are totally reliant on them. Anybody who comes into this work with animals has to have a passion. My other staff who work in the café or in the shop, or in administration, also have that passion and they love being connected to the thing that we do. One of the ladies who works in the gift shop has been with me for many years, and the first thing she does every morning is to go inside the aviary with all the big parrots and has them all down on her, feeding them. She absolutely loves those parrots.

*David Gill spent a tremendous amount of money in developing a zoo in Australia.*

In the last year since 2004 when I came back from Australia permanently, I have put everything into this park and I called for some very drastic and radical ideas and changes. The list of plans I still have for the park is endless. We're still working every day building new things, creating new things.

There's no way that I've stopped with my ideas and the ways that I can make it not only better for the animals, but more interactive for the people, so they can feel more emotionally closer to the animals.

Finally, I would like to stress that the key to the future is education for all ages. The focus is to try and get to as many people as we possibly can with our messages: for instance, highlighting that paper waste is one of the biggest reasons why we're having global warming. If we are cutting down trees that absorb carbon dioxide and producing way more carbon dioxide, we've got this dramatic imbalance going on. It's everybody making small changes that will make the difference. We have to change people as a group, so getting 250,000 visitors a year is my bit.

We have won the Lake District's top visitor attraction three times. In 2000, a Minister of Tourism actually came up to present me with the award. We have pulled back a few times and let other people have a go at it, and see what they can do, but I do believe we've got something special. I keep telling the staff we'll just keep working at it, because we're going to get better and better.

*At the time of its construction, 1993–4, David Gill, then a thirty-two-year old father of three, built the South Lakes Wild Animal Park with his own hands, and to this day still designs and builds all the facilities around the park – now with the help and assistance of the large staff.*

## *Vicky & Mike Brereton*

*Gleaston village is near Ulverston in the Lake District peninsulas of Cumbria. Gleaston-born, Mike Brereton and his Surrey-born wife, Vicky, own Gleaston Water Mill, which they have successfully restored, together with a complex of buildings: the water mill, Dusty Miller's, Pig's Whisper, Lile Cottage, the apiary, the Barleycorn suite, all of which draw visitors from far and near. Vicky and Mike were interviewed on 29 June 2006.*

There was a thriving community here from the Mesolithic Age. When Chris Salisbury, the archaeologist did the dig in 1993, he found eleventh-century Mesolithic flints underneath the contents of the watercourse. He started digging between the mill and Gleaston Castle and did some core samples and found there was quite a lot of evidence that from probably the back of the mill, right to just north of the castle, there was a shallow glacial lake. A gentleman from Reading University with a sort of *Time Team* equipment, said that it was quite likely that the lake did not just extend to the castle but it probably went all the way to Urswick Tarn, so from there to the mill there was one continual lake, rather like a mini-Windermere.

Vicky outside Gleaston Mill with geese. *(NW Evening Mail)*

We know the mill has been rebuilt on a previous site; when some archaeology was done inside the mill, we found a previous cobbled floor which is close to about a metre long. We think the original was two-storey and when you face the south side of the mill, the back of it is much older. The drying kiln is really old. We have currently been doing some more work in it, and it's quite likely that the drying kiln is part of the original two-storey building and possibly the only bit of the two-storey building that originally survived. Then they've added on the new mill, which is the bit on the north side, and then I think the outshot was added last.

Gleaston Mill was listed in King James's list of mills and it was rented to the mill for a pound. We have a statement in our deeds from 1663. Thomas Benson described how he worked at the mill when he was a young man. He said they got the new mill stones from Sandside and the local villagers had days when they worked on the mill race together, and the villagers went and got the stones and they stored them. He recalls how much they were paid in grain and drinks for their trouble.

That would put the mill building back to the late 1500s. We think it's fairly safe to say it was there in the days when the castle was built which puts it to the late 1300s or the early 1400s as the manorial mill for the castle. The final proof is the water course which starts off the beck at the back of the castle and comes around the fields down to the mill, which is also that sort of age.

The two rooms on the south of the building at the front were in pretty poor condition when we moved in; there were virtually no floors or ceilings. One room had been a room for malting barley. It had a slate skirting board; fairly typical of the time. The upper room was used for malting, while the lower room was probably the miller's office and store. Much later there had been 308 battery hens in these two rooms – a bit of a pong, and when we moved here the battery cages were still in there and they hadn't been used for twenty-odd years.

When we first came to the mill we did a lot of the jobs ourselves with the help of a team of venture scouts who cleared the two barley corn rooms of all the rubbish from the poultry days, and it was so bad in there we had to issue them all with face masks. There was nothing worth saving for it had all disintegrated into fine dust.

Now the two rooms are completely restored and carpeted and are known as the Barley Corn suite: they make little conference rooms, the upper rooms serving as offices. It's fairly 'high tech' because the office has got all modern equipment in it in terms of computing and IT facilities. There's a door goes through the tech. office into the mill on to a balcony; we call it a time door because you actually step through 400 years of technology.

In 2001 we decided to renovate the room next door to the mill; the building was not in good order and there had been a hayloft in it; it was totally derelict – no stairs, no floors. By Easter we had finished most of the building work, but by the end of February we got hit by foot and mouth disease which meant the building didn't open till the end of the summer. We decided we were going to open a gift shop and thus get better access to the mill while trying to encourage people into the mill, and also to make sure that when people came out of the mill they came through the gift shop.

We needed a theme. We've kept rare breed pigs at the mill so we decided to open a pig shop. The connection is with the holiday cottage (Lile Cottage), which is a converted pigsty and people took to that very favourably. When we had the archaeological digs on site, remains of pig bones from the eleventh century were found. Millers kept pigs usually for the lord of the manor because it was one of the duties of the miller to fatten up pigs. And, market research revealed that the pig was the second most collected animal after the elephant in the world. Finally, we chose 'Pig's Whisper' for the name of the shop. This comes from *Pickwick Papers* by Charles Dickens, where it says 'in a pig's whisper' which means in a grunt, a short period of time, in a flash.

We sell all sorts of gifts as well as pigs, including quite a lot of chutneys and jams and country things. We also have quite a lot of honey because we have the apiary on site so we sell honey on the Gleaston site and in the other villages. There is an interesting artefact in the mill room on the big long table about twelve feet long which is now covered with a pink carpet; it is, in fact, a curing table for ham so it's absolutely ideal to put imitation pigs on. In days gone by they used to cover the table in salt and saltpetre and water and make the brine, and rub the pigs with it, and then hang them up to cure, so it's a very appropriate use for it now.

Vicky displaying the home-made food outside Dusty Miller's. *(NW Evening Mail)*

Now we come to Dusty Miller's, which has turned out to be the focal point of the site. When we first started work on the mill, we saw the restaurant as being a bit of a prop financially, but now when people say they are going to the mill, they tend to think they are going to eat rather than going to look at the mill. Although we get a fair amount of visitors to the mill, nostalgia isn't what it used to be. People will now go in to see the observation bee hives and things that we have got in there but primarily do not come just for the mill. Visitors perhaps in the area will do, but not locals, and I think it's true to say if locals go round the mill once, they will not go round again in a great hurry. You can't change it that significantly, so the main reason that people will come is to eat, and for that reason we stay open all the year round, and we have found that we are often busier in February than we are in the height of the summer. We look after people who request coeliac and lactose-free diets; it's all freshly prepared food, pretty well local produce when we can get it.

We use local coffee and tea from Farrar's at Kendal and Richard Woodall's sausages, bacon and ham. Local farmers provide the beef for us. It's nice to be able to tell people that come in for Sunday lunch exactly which farm their beef has come from. We've got a little team baking who come in every day before we open. It seems to work well and be a good combination.

We know the café doesn't look like any other café in the area; it's not like an English café. An American came in today and said, 'Oh, isn't it cute?' It's been called quaint and like a cuckoo's nest. All the artefacts that are hanging up are pig lights from Henry Armer & Son, the agricultural merchants, and are very much in keeping.

Over the last eighteen years the whole of the mill has been restored and we have given a lot of thought towards our future plans. We've put all this work into the mill and we are passionate that the mill is retained as a working mill. We don't have any relatives that we choose to leave it to as they don't need us to make provision for them, so it is our current intention to leave the mill to a trust, and by that we mean the entire property as well. The big danger of leaving just a mill to the trust is that it could go bankrupt; we've seen that happen to so many mills. A mill is not self-sustaining for it cannot sustain on its own. We would therefore like to leave the entire property as a going concern to some form of trust. And, currently, we plan to set that trust up during our lifetime; we know then that the mill will be secure before anything happens to us, and we also know that we cannot sustain any more grants for it. We do have work that needs doing, particularly on the watercourse, and as individuals, there is no way that we could afford it, and there's no way we could make any money out of the grants. Obviously we wouldn't want to compromise the life we've got, so that is why we have decided to put the mill in the hands of a trust.

# SIX

# CIVIC VOICES

## Derek Lyon

*Derek Lyon was born in 1931 in Stoke-on-Trent. When he was eighteen months old, his Barrow-born parents brought him home and opened a chemist's shop in Hartington Street. Derek attended Holker Street Infants' School, St James's Junior School and the Grammar School in Barrow. He qualified as a solicitor in 1956, was Barrow's deputy town clerk for six months and Barrow's last town clerk from 1980 to 1988. He lives in Barrow with his wife, Vi. He was interviewed on 15 August 2006.*

The town clerk's post dates from the thirteenth century; there is a record of a town clerk at Nottingham in 1334. We can't claim that sort of ancestry in Barrow because we only obtained borough status in 1867, and that's when we had our first town clerk, so really I'm talking to you about a concept that existed for a long time but does not exist today. When I started, almost every town clerk was a solicitor or barrister but now the heads of boroughs are called chief executives – a wide range of professional backgrounds. Many chief executives these days are architects, planners or ex-housing people. The only people who are still town clerks are in effect clerks to the parish council, where the parish has taken on itself, as it's allowed in the law. The status of a town like Dalton, like Kendal, like Ulverston – they have all got their town clerks, really because of their historic background. I was asked what the difference was between a town clerk and a borough treasurer and I said that the town clerk was the shepherd of the flock and the treasurer was the little crook on his staff.

I want to make it absolutely clear that the councillors decide the policy of the council. They say what they want to do and it's our job as officers of the council to carry out those directives and it's the town clerk's job to see that any necessary work is done or in some cases, to tell the councillors that they can't do it because they haven't got the money, they haven't got the power, or it's illegal, or something like that. As one councillor once said, 'I know it's illegal but it's up to the town clerk to find a way around it.'

The job has changed immeasurably these days, for the worse, I think. There was a marvellous staff in the town hall when I was town clerk; everyone who was there did their job to the best of their ability and I got absolute help on anything I wanted to do – I was very fortunate with the people I was working with. I also thought because of my background and training, I had done every job that goes through a town clerk's department. I always did all the land charges and election stuff, and I was confident I could leave any job to any of the staff and they would do their proper job in carrying it out.

It's councils and committees that you get involved with when you are reaching the top of the tree, and that's the main job of the town clerk's department as I knew it: arranging the calendar of meetings, preparing the agendas for all these meetings, collecting all the supporting papers from all the departments to go with any agenda items that are going to come up, attending the meetings – some of them. I couldn't attend them all, but I attended the main, important meetings. Then, when those minutes are produced which says what the next committee has decided, seeing that that work is carried out. That's when you do rely on people who are committee administrators for that sort of work. I went to the main meetings which were council meetings, things like financial, general purposes committees, possibly housing, or transport in those days because we had our own bus fleet and therefore that was a big item in our expenditure. It was at committees that main contact was made with councillors who are all trying to say something to hit the headlines to get themselves into the *Evening Mail*, so that they can impress their constituents with the fact that they have spoken or that they have brought up their matter. The mayor is the chairman of the council meeting but in my time, although the mayor does it, it was my job to tell him what to say or to give the rulings on standing orders, because people are always trying to speak twice or try to bring something up which isn't on the agenda. You do get 'the slings and arrows' from some of the councillors if you stop them speaking.

I didn't enjoy council meetings in my latter days as town clerk because there was a group of them who were intent on trying to get rid of those who they thought were old stagers, who had been there a long time. We had all sorts of unruly behaviour and we had people who wanted to bring children in to nurse them because they couldn't leave them at home. However, we did have our lighter moments. There was one fellow who had a lovely way with words; he told us one day that he wasn't going to vote this through the top of his hat but was going to leave the matter in a basin [obeisance].

Council meetings, now open to members of the public, are the visible signs of activity. Behind the scenes, letters are being written to ministries, there are reports being prepared, the researching of legal opinions and making compulsory purchase orders. Other work involved traffic regulations, orders collecting rates, drawing plans for housing estates. Finance was always a bugbear – not my strong point anyway; we never had enough, we never will have enough. I always had strong admiration for Mrs Tait, who, during my time there was chairperson of finance and general purposes committee, which is the power committee. She was great, with marvellous political acumen and native cunning. Every year when it came up to estimates' time, the system at Barrow was that Mrs Tait as chair of finance would sit in the treasurer's office and then I would go in first with my estimates for the following year and the first time I ever went, she said 'Times are hard, there's not much money this year and I'm going to have to go through your estimates with a fine tooth comb.'. 'Oh Mrs Tait, mine are cut absolutely to the bone.' 'I'll have a look' she said and then she said 'Why do you get two *Evening Mails*?' I said, 'Well, we cut one up, that goes in the press cuttings – anything that affects the council – the other one circulates in the office in case there's anything anyone has missed and if it's of significance to whatever they're doing.' 'Oh' she said, 'No, no, strike one of those out' So, I lost an *Evening Mail*. The system was that I stopped in with every other head of department and I supervised them in a way. The next person comes in. 'Oh Jim, times are hard' says Mrs Tait, 'There's not much money about, I'll have to go through your estimates with a fine tooth comb.' 'Oh, Mrs Tait' says Jim, 'Mine is cut to the bone.' 'Oh' she said, 'Wait a minute, even the town clerk's had his estimates cut' – I'd lost one *Evening Mail*, he'd lost about ten thousand quid. But you could rely on Mrs Tait; if she was on your side, she was on your side.

Another aspect of my job which I found very interesting was that relating to elections. Rod Bedgar ran everything so smoothly in my time there. I was the electoral registration officer so that means that every year when you get that form through your door and you have to return it to make up the electoral register, you fill it in as to who is registered and entitled to vote at that time. We make up the electoral rolls from the returns that you send. Let me make it clear, here and now, neither I nor any other registration officer has ever put down the family dog or the baby of the house on the electoral registration form, and yet every year at election time, you will see the *Evening Mail* or a daily paper and there will be a picture of somebody going to the polling station towing a dog and saying 'My dog is on the electoral register so I'm taking him for his vote' or he carries a little baby in. We didn't put them on, you put them on, just because your dog happens to be called Sammy Smith, I don't know that's your dog, I just write the name and it goes on the national registration, nor do I know that Jasper Dunreary is a twelve month-old baby. If it's on the form, it goes on the list.

Every year someone fills in the forms incorrectly. Elections were a time of great tension for me, for I was the returning officer and it was up to me and my staff to conduct the elections and you would find it quite interesting to see the rules and regulations that there are to govern an election: the timetable, the ballot papers, requirement as to nomination papers, names of supporters, payments of deposits for general elections, notice of dates of election, places of voting, preparation of ballot papers, what can appear on them, the pink ballot papers, stamping instruments, ballot boxes, postal votes. This government has altered the system now and that has given licence to fraud. The postal vote system is in a shambles.

Then you come to the actual election day itself. Some places I've been, it was the custom there that the presiding officer took the ballot box home at night and then next morning turned up at the polling station, opened, and set up in operation. Here in Barrow, I think it was a better system that I inherited. We required people to come in at six o' clock or whatever it was to show that at least they were alive, before they picked up their ballot boxes with all the ballot papers in, and the stamping instruments, before they departed to the four corners of the borough to the various polling stations.

Then there could be a complication because most polling stations are public buildings like schools, parish rooms etc. I always used to say in my little preparatory

Derek Lyon has been a voluntary Lake District National park warden since 1968.
(*NW Evening Mail*)

talk on the night before: if you get to the polling station and there's no caretaker there, you break in, or if it's a nice morning you set up on the step. You must be open when the poll opens at seven o' clock because there's always somebody who comes in at seven o'clock – going on shift or coming off shift; same as when you've got about thirty seconds to closing time, three people come in and you are trying to fill the forms in to say how many ballot papers you have issued. I remember once when someone rang the town hall at the crack of dawn, and said, 'The polling station isn't open and there's no caretaker' and the reply was, 'Oh, I'll ring him up, he's probably slept in.' But, the caretaker was ex-directory and the struggle we had – even when a call was made to the General Exchange, stating that it was a national emergency, with the words: ' I demand to know this number.' The voice at the other end replied, 'You aren't going to get it' So I know that ex-directory does mean something. We sent someone round to wake him up.

If you have ever been a presiding officer or a poll clerk, you will know that it's the most boring job in this world and you get all the clowns that come in and say, 'You've got a good job.' You have then got to rush, fill your forms in and go back to the town hall with your ballot paper account which is the main thing, which states how many votes you've issued, how many ballot papers you've issued out of those that were given to you. I remember once we decided we would use a bus over Walney to pick all the polling booth people up from that side, coming to the town hall. Then someone comes upstairs within about two minutes of the poll closing, bangs his ballot box paper account on the desk – 'There you are Mr Lyon' and I asked, ' Where's your ballot box?' and he said 'Oh crikey, I've left it on the bus.'

Then you open the ballot boxes. There are two stages; first of all you have to verify, which means you empty all the boxes out – you just count them to make sure that those that have been issued have been returned, that there have been no extra ones thrown in or gone missing or if there's a ballot box gone astray. Then when you've verified them all, you then recount and allocate them to the various candidates and that's why when you are talking about thousands of votes, that's why a count lasts such a long time into the early hours of the morning if you do it straight away as we usually did here, at the close of poll. In South Lakeland, we brought the ballot boxes in and we had a policeman sitting on them all night and they all went in the morning because we had to bring them from so far away because it is a very big, widespread constituency is Morecambe and Lonsdale.

But here in Barrow we were able to declare at perhaps two or three o'clock in the morning, providing there were no re-counts and I had to adjudicate on whether there were any spoilt ballot papers. That's when a person has put two crosses for only one candidate or they put a cross through one of the names – what does that mean? Then there are people who write their names or their addresses, and that destroys the ballot paper. We also have to show that the magic stamp is on everything; that's a real black mark against the presiding officer if that gets through without a stamp.

Being a town clerk had its exciting moments like royal visits; there's always a lot of security issues and pre-planning like getting the right pen for the Queen to sign with – a Parker fifty-one, I think, with a certain sort of nib so she could sign the visitors' book in the mayor's parlour. I remember going with the mayor and mayoress to Berlin and the difficulties arising when we had to get the mayoral chain, worth a quarter of a million pounds, through customs.

Then came the chance to retire, and there was a great political change at the time and we had an early retirement scheme which I quickly took advantage of and so I finished in 1989 and I've been happily retired ever since, still living in my home town, and there is nowhere as far as I am concerned like the golden city of the north, which is Barrow.

## Hazel Edwards

*Hazel Edwards was born in 1947 in Barrow. She attended Roose Primary School and Barrow Grammar School for Girls, before qualifying as a teacher at Chester College. Initially she taught French at Victoria Girls' School and at reorganisation in 1979, she became Head of Modern Languages at Thorncliffe Comprehensive School. When Hazel took early retirement, she was Head of Learning Support and dealt with Special Needs. Teaching was only one of Hazel's achievements. She was a Conservative councillor for many years and a mayor of Barrow-in-Furness. Hazel is married to Keith and has two sons. She was interviewed on 7 June 2006.*

I became mayor in 1993 and it was very exciting. I'd been on the council for seventeen years. What saddens me today is people becoming mayors who haven't served on the council for any length of time. I think it's something that you earn and you have to know the area very well. My friend Ann Redhead was mayoress and we worked together very well. My children were too young and my husband didn't fancy being my consort, so he stayed at home. I was very proud to be mayor;

Hazel Edwards in Barrow Town Hall in the year she was Mayor of Barrow. *(NW Evening Mail)*

In the Council Chamber of Barrow Town Hall. Left to right: Rod Bedgar (principal administrator), the Mayor, Councillor Hazel Edwards (standing). Sitting from left to right: Tim Howes, legal services manager; Neil Anderton, senior committee clerk; and Diane Moore, committee clerk. (*NW Evening Mail*)

obviously it didn't change me and it was wonderful to meet people that you had only seen from a distance, getting into the shipyard, going to launches, meeting royalty, going to Buckingham Palace, meeting the Chinese Ambassador, people who you wouldn't meet under normal circumstances.

I met Princess Diana, had quite a chat with her. She landed by helicopter. It was quite a low-profile visit; she wasn't visible to the general public, other than the people who were at the dockside, because of security. A funny story: they'd just cut the grass and the princess landed by helicopter. We were wearing hats and the grass went everywhere, for which she apologised. The *Evening Mail* had to pick up the fact that both she and I had the same coloured outfit on with spots on. I'm sure they could tell (spot?) the difference. During my time as mayor we went to Buckingham Palace and saw the Queen, Prince Charles and the Queen Mother. In the past I'd met Prince Philip and the Queen in the town hall. Prince Philip thought that my husband was the councillor, not me.

I met Willie Whitelaw and I was quite impressed with him – a really nice man. I sat with him at a dinner and we chatted; very interesting. I met Margaret Thatcher during my years on the council and I met William Hague who previously I hadn't had much respect for. I thought he was very interesting, a genuine person, and Jeffrey Archer; I don't care for the man, but he's a good speaker, and I met Anne Widdecombe. I wasn't very impressed with her, but I think she is an intelligent and interesting lady.

When I was Mayor, John Hutton was our MP and we became good friends. Often we used to bump into each other in town and we used to get some funny looks, standing, holding conversations.

We did 500 events, one of which was unveiling the memorial plaque on Roa Island. I was quite touched by that and I get annoyed when I go to Roa Island and see people sitting on the memorial plaque. I think the Civic Society is a very important part of Barrow and I think it's growing actually in importance.

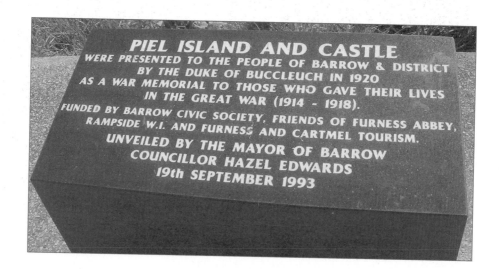

The plaque at Roa Island.
(Alice Leach)

We used to visit schools and turn up with the chains of office. The children learnt what the mayoralty was about; they all came into the Mayor's Parlour. We met captains from ships, we went with the army to Altcar; they were shooting rifles, machine guns and things, driving trucks. People were always surprised that it was a lady who turned up, because they expected a man to be mayor. One of the big events was the last event – the centenary in Blackpool Tower. All the mayors in the north-west turned up. We had the service in the tower circus and we drove in motorcade down the promenade.

One of the most important things was meeting the man on the street in Barrow and Dalton and going to all the little clubs and events. You don't realise how proud people are to have a mayor; it's not the person – it's the mayoralty – that's what people really want. There was some dispute at the time about cancelling the mayor out but I think it's grown from strength to strength, and I think my predecessor, Joyce Fleet, started that. She accepted far more invitations than previous mayors, and I continued that so people now include the mayor in their invitation lists so you get to most organisations in the area and I think that's important.

One of the highlights of my mayoral year was the first event. I had to go on my own to an RAF base to hand over a field gun that had been built in Barrow. I was told that I couldn't take anybody with me but they wanted me with the chains etc. Noel Davies was the manager of Vickers' Shipbuilding and he came in a plane. I really didn't know what I was going to, how formal it was and it was quite daunting, really. We had a big lunch, a march past of the army, after firing the guns. The man who stood next to me said, 'You have to remember that where you are sitting is where the Queen will be sitting next week'.

I feel I am a very lucky person. I'm determined, very interested in politics, still miss it – especially the planning side. I don't think people locally take enough interest in what's going on in the town.

*Hazel is now teaching at Furness College and has three classes, training teaching assistants. She covers schools between Barrow and Wabberthwaite.*

# Ian Smith

*Ian Smith was born in 1949 in Doncaster, South Yorkshire. He was educated at a local post-war Grammar School. On leaving school, he went on to University College London, to read law. He qualified as a solicitor in 1973 and became a deputy coroner in 1978. He has been a successful coroner for Barrow Borough and the South Lakeland District Council since 1990. Ian was interviewed on 27 October 2006.*

Mum was the traditional housewife, though if she'd lived in a different era, she would have gone to university. In the 1920s in Rochdale, she had to go out and work – in the cotton mill and in a grocer's shop. She met my dad on the pier at Blackpool – very romantic!

Dad went to school in Doncaster. I've got to say he didn't really fulfil his promise, if you're brutal about it, because he went to the grammar school and he didn't actually matriculate and he ended up as an apprenticed garage mechanic locally. I think that was a disappointment to his family [his own dad was a miner], but the war then came along and Dad went off into the RAF, ended up being a mechanic on Spitfire engines and when he came back, he found that he could do emergency training as a teacher, so he trained under the emergency training scheme for just over a year, so he finally fulfilled his potential.

So, Dad was a teacher and that was the one thing I knew I didn't want to be, and I ended up at school, reading languages. Half way through the sixth form I was doing French, German and Latin and suddenly it dawned on me that I didn't actually know what I wanted to do with my life. It was then that I decided to look for something different and law was something you could do from scratch, and that's why I did law, and even then, I didn't know what I wanted to do with it, so I ended up, really, being a solicitor by default.

I got my articles in a firm called Gamlens which was right in central London; it was in Lincoln's Inn. It was an old-fashioned family firm which dealt with trusts and all kinds of fairly basic legal work for people: lords at one end and illiterate immigrants at the other end, so I got a very good grounding, and it was a wonderful place to work geographically, and the architecture was wonderful.

In those days you could be very much a general practitioner which was what I was trained into and what I carried on doing really throughout my career. I qualified in 1973; as the years went by, the profession became more and more specialised so that the old fashioned family solicitor was less and less in evidence, and that was what I had enjoyed doing most, so it became a bit of a problem for me to continue to be a general practitioner: doing everything – conveyancing, wills, accident work, divorce – the whole lot.

I first came to this part of the country with an aunt and uncle when I was about eleven and it was then I discovered the wonderful Lake District and I must have had the thought that one day I would come back and live here. At the first opportunity I just looked for jobs in or around the Lake District and Barrow happened to be the first place where I was offered a post.

My career as a solicitor covered a wide range of cases but it is difficult to talk about individual cases because the people who were involved in them are still alive, still living locally, but I can speak about how the law works; for instance, family law. When I first qualified as a solicitor, divorce was frowned on. There were certainly innocent and guilty parties in the eyes of the law in the 1970s and there used to be a thing called a discretion statement so that if the innocent party (usually a woman), subsequently committed adultery, and I do mean subsequently – not during the course of the marriage – was supposed to file a thing called a discretion statement saying to the court, 'I'm sorry but I've committed a matrimonial offence as well, can I still have the divorce?' The judge then had the power to say, 'No you can't.' I think there were occasions when that was exercised. Now that's clearly moved on massively so that nowadays divorce is almost a paper exercise.

The law covers many aspects of ordinary life from the humdrum, to the dramatic, to the sad. In our society today, very young children are needed to give evidence in particularly upsetting cases, but it's done at a distance by video link so that they can be talked to by usually a police officer in a room somewhere where they're

Ian Smith is very much the local coroner but is still proud of his roots; the tie is from Yorkshire Cricket Club. *(NW Evening Mail)*

comfortable but what they're saying is relayed to the courtroom. There is no actual lowest age at which they can give evidence, but if they are very young indeed, then I guess what they had to say would have to be passed on at second hand by somebody like a police officer and confirmed by other evidence. Ten-year-olds, ten plus, can be accused in court, although this is not common. However, some people would say that a child under the age of ten can be very guilty of some horrible things, but the legal limit for actually being accused is ten. The actual age at which a young offender can be named may be a bit arbitrary, rooted in history. The age of majority is eighteen; you can drive a car at seventeen, get married at sixteen. You could say that the law in these areas should be brought up to date in one way or another by either increasing or lowering as the case may be.

I became deputy coroner in 1978 but that is a fairly low-key job; it's just that you are there as the deputy when the coroner is away. I became coroner in 1990 when Mr Wesley Ellison retired and if you like, I turned that into a full-time job by leaving the practice in 1995, so I've actually been coroner since 1990 but I've really been giving all of my energies to it since 1995.

I can tell you what my job entails briefly as follows: Any death has to be certified and a doctor can certify a death and the medical cause of death if the patient has been in his or her care, and there is nothing in any way other than natural about it; that, in fact, deals with about fifty per cent of all deaths. Anything other than that – it might be quite simply that doctors don't know why a patient has died – this is referred to me. In about eighty per cent or thereabouts of these cases, the cause of death becomes clear after a post-mortem examination, and that really is the end of the story at that point. This leaves a relatively small number of cases where an inquest – a public investigation, if you like – a public hearing is required; they are the sudden traumatic deaths or maybe, especially locally speaking, the deaths from industrial causes, in particular, asbestos-related diseases, going back to the shipyard.

From 1990 the area I covered was Furness and that meant precisely the old piece of Lancashire north of the sands. In 2004 the neighbouring coroner retired and the county amalgamated his area which is everywhere between Meathop and Sedbergh and even out to Garsdale and up as far as Grasmere. They merged that area with mine, so I now cover, on the extreme western side, the Duddon Valley with the river as the boundary, right across to the boundary with North Yorkshire and so it's effectively the Barrow Borough and South Lakeland District Council areas.

In my work there is in one sense no such thing as a typical day. I normally go into the office which is in the police station – that is by choice. I don't have to have an office there, but I go in and see what deaths have been reported – nearly all of them by the police, sometimes from the hospital. The first decision to be made is whether a post-mortem is needed. Sometimes a talk with a doctor will result in an agreement that the patient has actually died of a certain illness and the doctor will then sign the death certificate. Then it has to be decided whether a post-mortem is necessary, and if so, the path lab must be informed so that the mortuary and pathologists can carry out the post-mortem.

During the mid-morning there is usually not a lot going on, but towards lunchtime the results of the post-mortems start coming in and that is when it is time to make the next decision, whether they show the death was natural, in which case, paperwork has to be completed, but it's really just a matter of routine or it may show the death wasn't natural and that something else is involved, which means that an inquest has to be opened, which may happen later that same day.

The police or ambulance service are the first to hear of any sudden death, even if it's not particularly suspicious; the hospital ring in a large number of deaths and GPs ring in too. Very rarely you might get a call from a member of the public about a death of which you had no previous knowledge, but on the whole it's the police and the doctors who give the information.

I have worked on some dramatic cases: for instance, the Donald Campbell inquest. That was strange in one sense because normally an inquest involves people

Donald Campbell on Coniston Water in *Bluebird* in the 1960s. (*NW Evening Mail*)

who have recently lost a loved one; they're raw, all the emotions are still there, but Donald Campbell, of course, had died in 1967 and his body was only discovered in 2000 and by that time, a lot of the immediate raw emotions had healed to some extent. His daughter was at the inquest and she was older than her father had been when he died. We were able to piece together fairly accurately what had happened in physical terms (with the help of an expert), in the movement of objects across the water, and how even a slight movement in the boat on a lake that was rippled to some extent could lead to the boat becoming airborne. One particular strange fact that I remember is that when *Bluebird* was in contact with the water at 300-odd miles per hour, it was physically in contact with fourteen square inches. I stated at the inquest that in effect, it was like an aeroplane skimming along the surface of the water just touching it; technically it was still a boat, but only just.

Another dramatic and high profile case in which I was involved was 'The Lady in the Lake'. This attracted a huge amount of media interest. I can't add anything in the way of details as it's still such a local issue, and of course Gordon Park has been convicted and is serving a prison sentence.

I'm now fifty-seven years old and I'm enjoying what I do, and if that sounds a bit perverse, I do, because I don't go in with a Monday morning feeling. I go in positively wondering what the morning has got to offer and I'm never bored, which, I have to say, I was at the private practice; I mean conveyancing is not exciting and is not massively variable. I just don't know what I'm going into from one day to the next, so it's totally fascinating and how long I'll carry on doing it, I don't know. It depends on health and also the fact that the coroner's jurisdiction is being looked at by Parliament or at least by the Department for Constitutional Affairs, and there may be changes coming, but how big those changes will be remain to be seen. I think, I hope I will still be working in ten years' time as I don't really fancy just sitting with my feet up.

I have many interests: my mad passion is cricket; I go and watch and support Yorkshire because I was born in Yorkshire, and obviously, England. I love wildlife, which again is one of the reasons that I wanted to move here – for bird watching. I am interested in local history; I enjoy travelling and classical music, so I've got lots to keep me amused and to keep me interested – as well as my work.

## Gordon Hall

*Gordon Hall was born in Barrow in 1944 and attended local schools. Married to Brenda, he has two daughters, Annette and Marie, and one son, Geoffrey. He started work as an apprentice joiner at the age of fifteen. He took over the funeral business from his father in 1972 and is now a respected funeral director for Barrow and District. Gordon was interviewed on 9 March 2006.*

I first became interested in my father's work when I was a little boy, in the 1950s. We used to live over the office at 2 Montague Street, Barrow and I used to look out of the window and watch for the hearse and cars. Originally the joiner's shop was on the corner of High Street and Montague Street. We lived upstairs, and downstairs was the joiner's shop, where my father served his time. He started work as a boy, about thirteen. Subsequently, he bought the business from Mr Firth in 1938.

My father started the funeral business. We used to do funerals and joinery work, make the coffin and take it to the home. My father partitioned it off downstairs so we had access to the house. We had the chapel of rest there, on the corner of Montague Street. My father had the first chapel of rest in Barrow, and all the other people said it was stupid; a daft idea. As time moved on, it became a necessity. People used to keep the body at home; everybody had room then. Even the terraced houses had a parlour. Now with open-plan living, there's nowhere for them to go. We used to take a board to the house and wash and dress the deceased and lay them on the board and bring the deceased to our premises, and subsequently take the coffin to the house until the funeral. Now we go, often within the hour, and bring them back to do the necessary things and they go into the Chapel of Rest.

We always used to make our own coffins. We used to buy prepared boards of elm, sanded and cut to size. They came in bundles wrapped in metal bands, by train, and we kept them in the cellar, where it was damp, because elm needs to be kept damp. We took the bands off and weighted them down to keep them flat. When we needed a coffin, we'd get the boards and take them to the joiner's shop and make the coffin. Then we got the French polisher (the workshop was in Forshaw Street), and he polished them. Other businesses sometimes used varnish. Now we're too busy to do that and we buy coffins ready-made from a specialist firm. Most people do that. And, coffins have to be bigger now.

All the funeral directors used to use the same hearse and limousines, hired from Keat's Garage, (run by Harley's), at the top of East Mount. Initially we bought a Humber hearse, which I found at the back of a garage in Grange; it was stored away there. It was £160 about forty years ago, but we still hired the limousines.

In times gone by, people used to have to do everything themselves. The undertakers were usually joiners and came to measure the deceased and make the coffin. But the family had to do everything else – register the death, arrange the service, notices, flowers and the meal. Now, once we've got the instructions, we do everything and all they have to do is register the death. Sometimes people had a meal at home, but most had a sit-down meal, and in Barrow, nearly everybody used

Gordon Hall. *(NW Evening Mail)*

to go to the Co-op Café. Now there's much more choice of hotels, etc., and most people have a buffet.

Flowers used to be all wreaths. Since oasis came in you don't have to make wreaths with moss and wire any more. People now often choose arrangements in oasis, and you can have any kind of flowers you want, instead of only the ones in season.

You no longer see the big, ornate gravestones and memorials; there aren't the craftsmen to do that now, and people haven't the money. They're much simpler and they are done by machines. The machine cuts everything out. There are certain rules in the cemeteries, and the Church Commissioners have rules for churchyards.

People used to be very formal; they all wore black. Now it is more relaxed. Curtains used to be closed and neighbours would stand at the door. I remember the funeral director in a swallowtail coat and top hat. I wear a black jacket and striped trousers, and a black overcoat if it's cold. Sometimes we are still asked to walk in front of the hearse, but only down the street.

The role of the funeral director is to help people with a situation they can't cope with. When somebody dies at home, we go there within the hour, unless they want to wait a little longer, and from then on we deal with all aspects of the funeral. We take all the details from the family, then go back to the office and make the arrangements to suit them. We like to think we treat them as we would like to be treated ourselves.

We then contact the cemetery or crematorium and the minister, and arrange a suitable time for the funeral, deal with the paperwork, arrange for the doctor to complete the certificate. The family would have to register the death; that's all they'd have to do. We then co-ordinate the cemetery or crematorium, the service, the florists and the caterers. Then our own drivers and staff collect the deceased from the home, nursing home or hospital and we take care of the deceased from then till the time of the funeral. We make the deceased presentable for the family to come and see them and dress them in their own clothes or a gown.

The family choose whatever funeral they want – just a hearse, or it may be very elaborate with a horse-drawn hearse and three or four cars. We close the coffin about an hour before the funeral, which gives everybody the opportunity to see the deceased for the last time.

We go to the house and co-ordinate everybody, get them into the right cars and go to the church or crematorium. There are two of us at the funeral, myself and my daughter; she looks after the family and I look after the bearers and the deceased, so that the relatives aren't left on their own, wondering what to do. We take the coffin into the church; we have a bier to take the coffin to the door, and then carry the coffin up the aisle. If we have a large person we usually take the coffin all the way on the bier. We have had a special bier made for us, higher than the normal ones, so the bearers don't have to stoop as they're going up the aisle.

When the church service is finished we go to the crematorium for the final service. Following that, we take the mourners home or to the hotel. More people go straight to the crematorium now; religion's out of fashion for many. Most funerals used to take place in church, but nowadays we get more people wanting a secular funeral. We have a gentleman who conducts them for us: poems, readings, some music and a eulogy. It's more a celebration of life.

Hearses are smaller now; they used to be coach-built onto a chassis. The car from the manufacturers was built up to the driver's part of it; then they put on the hearse body. Modern funeral vehicles are different. We had the last of the totally dedicated vehicles. We have now changed them. We have had Daimlers from 1970 to 1992. We've moved on to six-door vehicles; they're Daimlers but basically cut in half and extended, which gives the basic seating capacity for six. For the hearse they build a body on to the chassis. The old ones were Rolls-Royces. I've got a passion for Rolls-Royces. I have five now, from 1926 to 1936; we use them for weddings.

The business has changed a lot; it's much less formal. I like it to be a closer relationship with the clients so they don't feel a great divide. We like to keep it on a personal basis. I prefer to be called Gordon and my daughter prefers to be called Marie. We like to keep a friendly relationship with our clients and put them at ease. There are a few who like to be formal. But we do maintain high standards at all times.

One of the first funerals I conducted when taking over the business in 1972 was £116. That was for a hearse, eight limousines, a service in St Mark's, and a burial in Ulverston cemetery. Now you're looking at £1,800 to £2,000, depending on peoples' needs. We act for our clients as banker because we pay out on our client's behalf all disbursements and then send them the final account. This includes the coffin and arrangements for the funeral, collection of deceased from house or wherever, certificates, provision of hearse and cars, church fees, cremation fees, purchase or opening of a grave, subsequent burial of ashes, doctor's fee for the completion of certificates, minister's fee for conducting the service, church fees, notices in the papers, flowers and catering.

In the old days, nobody thought of asking how much a funeral would cost, you just did it and had to sort it out afterwards. When I go to arrange a funeral I ask them what they want and we sort it out then. When they decide on the type of funeral, we give them a written estimate before the funeral so they know what the costs are and have the opportunity to vary things if they want to. In Barrow now an obituary notice for one night is £70 [in the *Evening Mail*]. For two notices and a thanks notice it is £200–£220. Costs are high. We are a unique business in that we take people on trust. We don't have a signed agreement.

Funeral plans pay at today's price and we maintain it for you, but there may be a slight shortfall, due to rising costs. They are transferable, so if you have been living in a different place, another director can take over. We do not hold this money, it is held in a central fund.

Ashes are received from the crematorium in a plastic urn. We put them in a suede bag with a drawstring. People can scatter them in the cemetery or in a favourite place, bury them in a family grave, scatter them on the grave or purchase a space and bury them in a cremation grave in a churchyard or crematorium grounds.

# John Hutton MP

*John Hutton, Secretary of State for Works and Pensions has been MP for Barrow and Furness since 1992. He was born in London in 1955. John was interviewed on 7 July 2006.*

My parents weren't academic. My father, who had left home when I was twelve years old, had worked as a bailiff for the Water Board and as a labourer on a number of construction projects. My mum was an orthoptist; she trained after the Second World War and worked for the National Health Service for most of her life. My dad was more political than my mum. He had been a member of the Labour Party for a long time as had his grandfather before him; it was a family thing, being a member of the Labour Party. My parents weren't active politically and I don't think my dad had ever stood for office although I do remember him going to meetings.

I never planned a career in politics; I wanted to be a lawyer and I succeeded in achieving that goal. I was very happy teaching at the University of Northumbria as Senior Law Lecturer. I loved it; I had a young family and that's what I thought my life was going to be. Then something happened to cause me to change my career – Mrs Thatcher, she did it for me. I wanted to do something to stop what I thought was a really bad period for our country. Yes, it was Mrs Thatcher that brought me into active politics, because I thought we were returning to the mass unemployment of the 1930s and this was something we thought we would never see again in the UK. Britain was becoming more divisive and the gap between the rich and poor was growing. I didn't like any of these things and I wanted to do what I could do to stop them.

Before I came to Furness I had stood for Parliament once and I had stood in the European Parliamentary Elections in 1989 and I really wanted to go to a winning seat where there was a prospect of winning. There were people in the Barrow Labour Party who had got to know me during the European Parliamentary Election Campaign and they said to me, 'Look, would you be interested in standing for Barrow?' I definitely was, because I always thought this would be a seat we could win back and we did win it back in 1992, I'm very glad to say.

I found out a lot about how parliament and government works during my time on the Select Committee for Home Affairs. However, my parliamentary career wouldn't have taken off without the support of my first wife, Rosemary and my family.

My first impressions of the north-west were that it was a beautiful part of the country with the most extraordinary history; we were right at the beginning of the Industrial Revolution, and we helped shape it. The communities that I began to have contact with had fantastic social and economic and political history and I was delighted and thrilled that I had any role to play at all in it. The world has moved on in the last twenty years and it's my view that our country is changing more quickly than in any time since the Industrial Revolution which happened in towns like Barrow. Now we are experiencing a change very dramatically but my affection for this part of the country hasn't changed and my sense of a positive future is more strongly held than it was twenty years ago.

John Hutton MP on Election Night. *(NW Evening Mail)*

My constituency includes all of Barrow going up to Askam and Dalton and Ulverston and all the area between Ulverston and Dalton; I am MP for Barrow and Furness. I don't get to see as many constituents as I would like, although we do have a growing contact through e-mail with people. We have a website and we get a lot of contacts in that route. I do regular surgeries, I've just had one today [7 July 2006]. People stop me in the street or when I go shopping and tell me what they think about what's going on but you can never have enough contact. It would be lovely to say I have all the time in the world for them, but it's not possible.

I think what matters is the extent to which you can keep in touch with the heartbeat of your own constituency, and I try very hard to understand what people are saying to me and what they are thinking and so on. I think when it comes to benefit reform, I think it's quite correct – we have a very large number of working age adults claiming incapacity benefits; one in five of the working population, a very high number, so it's really important that we get the reform to work for them. The whole purpose of the reform is to give them the opportunity to get back to work, to contribute to the community and to make provision for themselves and their families. It's not about cutting benefits or being punitive – people aren't to blame for the problems they are in, it's the system that's let them down. One constituent has stated: 'If you are doing nothing and getting money, then some people feel then what's the point?'

This statement underestimates the basic human impulse to provide for yourself and your family, which I think is very strong. Most people in my constituency when I have spoken to them say, 'Look, I want to work, no-one gives me any help, I don't get any special help with my health care problems whatsoever.' I don't believe that people are happy to stay on incapacity benefit indefinitely because it means that they are going to be poor and socially excluded and they don't want that. Another constituent has said: 'I know lots of people with illnesses who love to work but can't. They're the ones I worry about.' I too, worry about these people. One of the fundamental objectives of the Labour Movement has always been the right to work, but not just for able-bodied people; the right to work has got to extend to people who are disabled too. Regrettably, the Welfare State has never helped people who are disabled to get back into work and that is a big challenge for us now and I think we should get on and do it. I should also add that it's not part of our policy to put people who are disabled under stress at all; this is one of our extending new opportunities of helping and supporting. It's not about making people take up jobs they can't physically do.

We have different problems here in Furness from many other parts of the country, but we also have similar problems: the economy, young people getting started in life, schools, hospitals. These are common concerns right across the country but we haven't experienced some of the other changes that have affected other parts of Britain, but neither have they gone through in the last fifteen years what we have gone through, that is, rapid change in our industries.

The regeneration programme is progressing, although I worry sometimes about how quickly we are succeeding in reaching it. I think the project to revitalise the dock area is really important. I think that has the prospect to open up a new economic opportunity for the Furness area and we've got to seize that opportunity, because they don't come that very often. I think the dock redevelopment is probably one of the most significant changes that will impact for the better; for the community of Furness, probably for a generation.

Barrow Civic & Local History Society is concerned that in the plans for the marina and the necessary demolition of nearby buildings, that the site of Barrow village, built on the site of an original Furness Abbey grange, will be lost if not professionally recorded for posterity. I can assure Barrovians that we will do all we can to properly preserve and record our local history, and when it comes to major re-developments like the dock, they've got to be done sensitively so that we don't lose the very important part of who we are and what we are, and where we've come from, and all of these buildings are a very important part of our local history which we should try and hold on to as much as possible.

Tourism can be important to Barrow and Furness, but we need a proper infrastructure locally to support the arrival of more tourists. I don't think we've necessarily got all of that part in place. I think we've got a tremendous industrial history; the history of Barrow is the history of the Industrial Revolution, and we also have the medieval history of Furness Abbey and its legacy. We should exploit these to full advantage.

The South Lakes Wildlife Park attracts the largest number of tourists while many visitors and locals visit the Dock Museum. If we are going to create any new museums they have got to be able to stand on their own two feet; they've got to be able to survive economically. The work will have to be done; a business case for those will have to be proven before we could successfully embark on these projects.

I would sum up my contribution to the Furness community as follows: I try to work very closely with people locally, to build a proper, decent future for the economy. I just hope it's been a productive relationship. I feel it has been, but we still have a lot more to do and I really want the opportunity to go on and complete the project now because I think we are at a pivotal moment now with a lot of these projects. We all know that our community has changed enormously in the last fifteen years; it's going to change even more, and we've got people locally who have done a brilliant job, who understand the nature of the challenge, and the changes we face and I think we can all work closely together – well we work closely together, and we have a very good chance of getting the result we want. I'm absolutely convinced we have a tremendously exciting future.

We've got a vibrant shipbuilding industry still in the community and I've no doubt that will be the heart of the future community, but we've got many opportunities now to adapt to new redevelopments which I think are very important. We have good opportunities and a whole range of industries; the service sector and tourism as well. We've got a brilliant future, we just have to be prepared to take it and I think people locally want all this regeneration work to be a success, and I'm confident it will be.

*Prime Minister Gordon Brown made John Hutton MP Secretary of State for Business Enterprise and Regulatory Reform in his Cabinet, 28 June 2007.*

## Margaret Crawford

*Margaret Crawford was born in Salford in 1923. She gained a degree in Social Administration at Manchester University. In her early career she worked in Manchester and Lancaster. Margaret was interviewed on 23 May 2005.*

I came to Barrow from Lancaster in 1952 for a whole fifteen pounds a year increase in salary and I was appointed Deputy in the Housing Department, and in 1965, Housing Manager when Harry Addison retired. It was a tough time for people when I arrived in Barrow in 1952. The first spread of post-war houses had been built but people who had served during the war came back, being married during the war or soon after and there were plenty of large families needing houses; there were about 2,000 or more on the housing list. I can remember when I first came to Barrow, if you said you were a married couple with children aged four and two,

Family butcher on the corner of Blake Street and Duke Street. *(James Melville/Alice Leach)*

living in a one-bedroomed Barrow Island flat, you wouldn't have been considered for a number of years. Priority had to be given to people who had not got their own private accommodation. If you were living in a flat or a house, however overcrowded, you could shut your front door on yourself – you had privacy. If you were living in either a rented property, or most frequently probably living with relatives or parents, that was where the priority was because you didn't have your own space, your own privacy.

A lot of council houses were built at this time because Barrow only had 874 houses before the war because of the Depression. It was very interesting that in 1920–1, they built 181 houses, mostly on Devonshire Road – sixty-eight or so and on Walney, I think about 181. But from 1921 to 1932, not a single council house was built and I understand that at some point there were up to thirty houses boarded up because they couldn't let them because people could not face up to the rents, however low those rents were. That was when unemployment figures were about fourteen per cent.

I seem to remember Ormsgill tenants' rents were something like £1 13s a week. People could pay in the office, or if they preferred, at the door. The advantages of door-to-door collecting meant that apart from trying to get the money in the easiest way for people to pay, you were able to keep an eye on your houses. You could see which, if any, were neglected, which were perhaps where people needed some help and advice; houses had got verminous at times. On the other hand, you also wanted to have any necessary repairs done. And, if you were collecting the rent, nobody knew whether you were going in the house to have a talk with somebody whose housekeeping was not up to standard, or whether you were going to collect the rent, or merely to look whether a window frame needed repairing. Rents increased steadily over the years. When I retired in 1982, three-bedroomed houses had rents of about ten pounds a week

There was always a problem with rent arrears, but I had to differentiate between the people that could pay, but who went to the pub on the way home on a Thursday night when they got their wages and there was nothing to give their wives, and the people who were in difficulties, and that was where the social element of my work would come in, trying to help people perhaps to budget or to aid those in need of further help from other agencies. I didn't just want to say 'Pay your rent or you'll be out' – I was concerned. If ever I had to reach the point of an eviction, I felt I had failed. It was the last resort. Occasionally you got people that just did not think that trying to pay one's way mattered. Threats of eviction had to be given and normally that was enough. It was very, very rare to have to evict anybody and that was extremely unpleasant. And then of course, after 1977 and the Housing Homeless Persons' Act, we in the housing department had to re-house these 'homeless persons' in the twenty-bedroomed hostel that we had for homeless people.

Another story relating to rent arrears: In 1955, Barrow Rugby, under the leadership of their captain, Willie Horne, went to Wembley for the Challenge Cup Final. Many special trains were filled with fans. My main concern was that every week the books had to be balanced. A weekly graph showed rent arrears and the week Barrow went to Wembley, we'd shot off the graph completely. You always got

Tay Street with J. Gill's milk float and a midden which visitors thought was a big bandstand, not somewhere to empty ashes. *(James Melville/Alice Leach)*

it at Christmas and Easter where the arrears would go up a bit, and then after two or three weeks they would come down, but this shot right off the graph and of course the aftermath of that – it would be eighteen months or two years later when the government auditors came auditing our accounts, and wanted to know what had happened to our rent arrears during that particular week in 1955, and we had to explain that Barrow had gone to Wembley!

Every type of person lived in council houses. You had the ones that looked just like a walking furniture showroom – you wouldn't have dared sit down for fear of disturbing a cushion and they had beautiful gardens. In the main, the houses were thoroughly pleasant, homely places. When the Scotch Buildings in Hindpool were being cleared, there were those flats that were absolutely immaculate and beautiful and most of these tenants were absolutely delighted to have the opportunity of

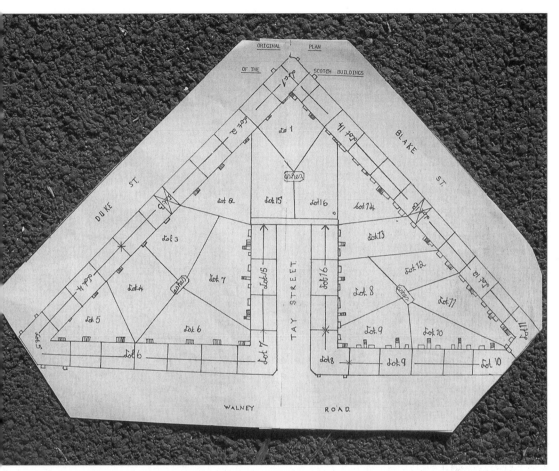

A copy of the original plan of the Scotch buildings from Cumbria Record Office, Barrow.
*(James Melville/Alice Leach)*

going into a new, not necessarily newly built, house but a modern one. However, when you got down to the end of the houses that you couldn't get in during the day, you went at night to a fourth-floor flat up a darkened stone staircase with no lights. On one occasion I found an old man there who'd just got back from the pub. He had a bed for a dog but he didn't have one for himself. So, in cases like that we would try to collect furniture to help those kind of people and try to teach them some sort of pride. It was always a sad duty of the Housing Department to house anybody that no-one else wanted.

*The Scotch Buildings, referred to by Margaret Crawford, were built by Smith and Caird, from Dundee, for the Haematite Steel Company, 1871–2. These buildings were similar to the tenement flats they had previously constructed in Scotland. The flats were therefore always known as the Scotch Buildings. They were badly damaged in the Second World War and demolished in 1956.*

A funny incident occurred at the time when the *Resolution* and the nuclear submarines were being built. The Ministry of Defence had two crews, Port and Starboard, and they wondered whether we could provide council houses – married quarters on North Walney and on the Griffin. I think up to 100 houses were allocated as married quarters, and I remember the commander of one submarine who was fairly new to Barrow came very politely to introduce himself – all beautifully done up in his uniform – and he came into my office, which was virtually often like a second-hand showroom filled with furniture for people that we wanted to re-house. This particular day one of my staff had parked a double-bed mattress in my office as they really couldn't find anywhere else to put it. The commander came in and took his naval cap off and laid it down on the side of this double-bed mattress without batting an eyelid.

Police Crime Prevention Officer, Sharon Livesey (left), after presenting the *Evening Mail* bouquet of the week in 2005 to Margaret Crawford at Barrow police station. (*NW Evening Mail*)

Since I came to Barrow in 1952 there have, of course, been changes in housing. From 1962 every house started off with central heating and houses have been modernised, peoples' standards of living having increased. Barrow has had its ups and downs as regards employment, but nothing compared to what it had between the wars. We've lost the big Vickers and the steelworks and Listers – we used to provide accommodation for key workers who were coming to work in new factories. I remember housing people from Bowater Scotts and Listers. Barrow never had the slum clearance that many towns needed and we never had back to back houses. I remember when ministry officials came up; they were always amazed at the width of our back streets. And, Barrow has a high incidence of owner-occupation, far in excess of anywhere else in Cumbria or the north-west.

Improvement grants were given for the older houses and to a very high level so that people on the whole have taken a great pride in their houses in Barrow, and people have liked living in the town centre and that's why we developed the houses on Scott Street when we had to clear some properties there. And, although some people from those houses were happy to go to Walney, others wanted to stay where they were and I remember doing a jigsaw of trying to take part of the street down and moving people into those, while new flats were being built, so that if they really wanted to stay in the same area, they could do so and I think that has helped keep Barrow town centre alive. I remember Ministry officials coming up when the flats in Holker Street near the station were being planned, and we were also building on Walney, and they couldn't understand why on earth we were wanting to develop a site there when people could have nice houses within yards of a sandy bathing beach on North Walney. I had to explain to them that I knew what would happen and it did. If somebody as much as sneezed in those flats, somebody would be down to see whether there was any chance of getting that flat when that person passed away.

From about 1980, council house tenants could buy their homes. When I retired, the houses were priced at £5,500. I think about just under 200 had been sold at that time, but since then a lot more have been sold, about two or three thousand. Of course, building has stopped.

*Margaret Crawford retired from her job as Head of the Housing Department in 1982. She has since been on the management committee of the Citizen's Advice Bureau and still does voluntary work in the police station for Neighbourhood Watch and the Victim Support Group.*

# SEVEN

# MISCELLANEOUS VOICES

## Betty Wilkinson & Wyn Dawson – the Bon-Bon Ladies

*Betty Wilkinson and Wyn Dawson are both now in their mid-seventies. Betty Wilkinson was interviewed on 31 May 2006.*

Wyn and I first met in Marks & Spencer's where I had worked for twenty years and Wyn for ten. In 1964 we decided to go into our own business, to rent a sweet shop in the Ritz block of buildings in Abbey Road. The Ritz Cinema opened in 1936. The shops were occupied by the photographer, Maurice Wright, Hadwin's Grange Travel, the optician, Harry Bellafontaine and Charles (Chas) Boyle, who had the Bon-Bon sweet shop, and this is the shop we rented until we were forced to move to Paxton Street in 2004 when the cinema and the shops were demolished.

All the original fixtures and fittings from 1936 were there when we took over – good solid oak. We worked a seventy-two-hour week; nine to eight on weekdays and two to eight on Sundays. We built up the trade in this confectioner's and tobacconist's, selling old fashioned sweets: milk gums, cherry lips, pear drops, raspberry ruffles, Uncle Joe's mint balls, liquorice comforts, Pontefract cakes, aniseed balls and old fashioned black bullets.

Cinemas like the Ritz were in their heyday and as picture goers were queuing to go in, they had to pass our shop and they would drop in to buy sweets, cigarettes, cigars or tobacco. In the early days there were two matinees and two shows a night. The trading was good then and Holker School with its 600 pupils was close by. Every lad had a 'tanner' or 'two bob' in his pocket.

We sold numerous brands of cigarettes and tobacco like Baby's Bottom and Parson's Pleasure. This was an age when every man seemed to smoke a pipe. One customer is still alive at 105 years of age; he had smoked thick brown twist tobacco from the age of twelve, and his daughter still comes into the shop to buy it from the Bon-Bon in Paxton Street. Another customer bought snuff – she had been in service and had not been allowed to smoke cigarettes. She still bought snuff from the Bon-Bon until a few days before her 100th birthday.

There were 15,000 people employed at the shipyard in those days and a percentage of them were our regular customers and we had people travelling from work to Askam and Millom on the train which they caught at the railway station which was nearby. The baths was down the road so all in all, trading was good as the position was so central. Wyn and I managed between us and we didn't have to

Betty Wilkinson (left) and Wyn Dawson outside the Bon-Bon, Abbey Road. *(NW Evening Mail)*

employ anyone although Wyn's husband, Harry, used to help. We owe part of our success to the fact that we had been M&S trained.

There was a lot of opposition in the town when Barrovians were told the Apollo Cinema and the adjoining shops were to be demolished. [Emlyn Hughes' House now occupies the site of the former cinema and shops in Abbey Road. The late, famous footballer was born and bred in Barrow.] Over 1,000 people in two days signed a petition to save the Bon-Bon and there was tremendous support from the *Evening Mail*. Nevertheless, Barrow lost an Art Deco building and we had to move from a tree-lined road to a back alley in Paxton Street, near the indoor market.

We took all the fixtures and fittings with us because we wanted it to be as much like the old place as possible. The Bon-Bon is still the same, only smaller. Now we have granddads that we served as little boys. Youngsters from Alfred Barrow School come in with twenty or thirty pence; it's not supermarket trade, but every customer is important. One lady came in the other day and said, 'It just smells like Abbey Road; how did you manage it?'

Betty and Wyn Dawson behind the counter of the Bon-Bon. *(NW Evening Mail)*

Wyn and I have spent forty-two years working together. We serve as we would like to be served. We always have time to listen. We just hope this spirit is carried on after our day.

# Sean McCusker: 'A Sometimes Bitter Pill'

*Sean McCusker was born in 1920 near Omagh in Northern Ireland. He was educated by the Christian Brothers and served an apprenticeship, doing a combined course at the Technical College at Belfast. After some years as a chemist, he emigrated to England with his wife Betty and their six children.*

My first job was in Keay's chemist, Barrow, where I worked for two years with the intention of buying the shop until I realised the shop was going to be knocked down for redevelopment. I realised this was not going to work out. However, there was a shop for sale on Barrow Island which I bought from Mr Spedding in 1963. The Barrow Island people were all wonderful – very friendly. When the trouble started in Ireland I got slightly apprehensive in case some of the boys from the army there had been killed. I never had any reaction at all. Some Barrow Islanders did not have a very healthy diet; there was one old, retired couple who used to walk past the shop every day with twelve to fourteen packets of crisps. People often came to me with medical questions rather than go to the doctor's surgery. I felt at times I was the doctor of Barrow Island.

Thalidomide was being prescribed at this period. We got regular reports from Sweden and Germany that this drug was causing problems, but we were told there was no evidence to back this, so 'keep on taking the pills'. I regret very much that I did not keep this literature. It was just a cover up to make more profits. Happily, there were no incidents of side effects from thalidomide in Barrow.

Talking about drugs, primarily there was Black and Green that everyone had at this time; then followed amphetamines which people thought cured everything including depression. One old lady came into the shop and said she had been to the doctor's and told him all her troubles and she thought he was listening. However, when she went to the chemist's shop and saw three different people all getting Black and Green tablets, she came to the conclusion that her doctor had not been listening.

Nowadays you hear a lot about people being 'stressed out'. Barrow Island people didn't suffer from stress – I think it's an upmarket thing.

I met many interesting characters. One customer came with a prescription for a sore leg. Then he asked for something for his sore head and was disgusted when the doctor told him the medicine would also help his head problem. Stupid man! How could leg medicine help his head – two different parts of his body? This customer's home help said he used to drink what he was ordered, stand on one leg and hop vigorously to get the drug down into his leg! I was very sorry to leave Barrow Island; it was home from home really – a real village atmosphere. I didn't spend a lot of time in the Roose Road shop for I had a manager.

After thirty years I retired aged sixty-five years on the thirty-first of July and started as a locum on the first of August. A pharmacist had died in one of Murray's shops and they had difficulty getting help. I enjoyed working as a locum. You didn't have any bills to worry about at the end of the month; you just put your money in your pocket; you could just walk out the door and forget about it. No stress – that

Sean worked at this chemist's shop on Barrow Island from 1963 to 1993. *(John McCusker)*

word again. I worked in Barrow, Ulverston and Arnside. I have been asked if there is a drug problem in Barrow. I didn't really encounter this till after I retired. It's fairly serious for the size of the town. There would be drug addicts in every day, mostly on methadone.

Lastly, I have to say that I'm not a great believer in alternative medicine; I'm not disposed towards it. I loved my work, meeting people and enjoyed their appreciation for everything I did for them.

# Alan Wright: 'A Clean Sweep'

*Alan Wright was born in Barrow in 1965 and was educated locally. He now lives in Dalton with his wife, Linda. Alan was interviewed on 21 September 2006.*

I worked in Vickers for eleven years as a welder until 1992. That was when the Berlin Wall came down and everybody started getting laid off. Most of the night shift were put back on to days, which I couldn't stand. I was in the pub one night having a drink and someone asked me if I fancied chimney sweeping for a living. It just started from there, really.

My business started up from scratch by myself; a lot of people are under the impression that it's a franchise I run, but actually, it's my own business. I think I'm the only full-time chimney sweep in the area. I cover most of South Cumbria: Barrow, Dalton, Ulverston, Kirkby and further afield.

In my work as a chimney sweep, I prefer to do it the old way with rods and brushes, but I do have a vacuum. When you use the old rods and brushes you get to know the feel of certain chimneys and get to know what sort of state they're in. A lady from Askam, in Steel Street, asked me to open up her fireplace; more and more people are wanting this done. I set about this job by chipping the plaster away to uncover the original sandstone surround. I then obtained some Burlington slate for the hearth and cut it to shape. It seemed a shame to stand a gas fire on this for the patterns in the slate were so beautiful.

On another day in Askam, this time in Duddon Road, on a calm day, that was, to begin with, I was working on a cat ladder by a chimney-stack. Suddenly, with the turn of the tide, the wind got up, and it blew the big extension ladder about five feet sideways and came to rest against the guttering bracket five feet away. I couldn't reach it from the cat ladder and I couldn't get off the roof. On the back of the roof there was an old skylight which, fortunately, was open. I lifted it up and lowered myself into the loft, landing on the loft floor. Then the skylight fell down, shattering all the glass, smashing above my head. There was a proper door in the loft with stairs – but the door was locked. The customer came up stairs shouting, 'Who's there, what are you doing in here?' I banged on the door and was released, but I had to repair the roof.

The worst part of my job is when it is a wet and windy day and I have eight or nine chimneys to sweep and I turn up at the last one standing on a cream carpet, and I'm dripping wet with black rain dripping from me and the lady of the house looks at me as much as to say, 'Are you coming in here dressed like that?' and I'm thinking if she wants her chimney cleaning she's going to have to let me come in. Sometimes you get an awkward chimney – most chimneys have a dog-leg on them but some go up at such an angle, I have to go up into the loft.

Chimneys sometimes collapse. I can remember one in Hartington Street in Barrow; it was the tallest chimney-stack in the street. I was working at one chimney in the back room and the lady was in the front room, watching *Coronation Street*. Suddenly there was such a clatter and rumble as my rods got to a certain point. I was looking at one chimney and a big pile of bricks came clattering down the front

Alan dressed to bring good luck to a happy wedding couple. *(Linda Wright)*

room chimney and the lady of the house was covered with a big cloud of house brick dust. All she said was, 'Don't worry about it, my husband has been talking about getting that stack sorted out for years.'

When I first started sweeping chimneys, I was asked every week to appear at weddings; according to tradition, this was supposed to bring good luck to the bridal couple. My first one was on Barrow Island and I had scouted round and got all the bits and pieces: waistcoat, pocket-watch and things. I got some strange looks from people walking to the church with my rods and poles, brushes and top hat. One of the family had arranged it and I just hid round the corner, and when they came out, I wished them all the best and gave them a little figure of a chimney sweep and they took one or two photographs.

One of the most interesting jobs I have been asked to do is working on *Gondola*, a plush, rebuilt Victorian steam-powered yacht, on Coniston Water. I am employed from April to the end of October each year. Every Friday I travel to Coniston. First of all, I remove the soot from the boiler floor. Then I clean eighty tubes by putting rods through each one, each being ten feet long. I check there's nothing out of

The *Gondola* on Coniston Water. *(Alan Wright)*

place and sweep the funnel. Lastly I bolt the boiler panel back up and then it is ready to fire up. One day I was working in the tank and I popped my head up with a bag of soot. Now, there's a big timber on the end of the jetty and there was a lady leaning against it with her eyes closed. On opening her eyes she saw me and got a shock as I did, on seeing her. She had been meditating, thinking there was no-one to disturb her. Apparently she had been attending a meditation week in Grizedale Forest. There followed an interesting conversation about the best walks in the Lake District. I advised her to read Wainwright's books with his excellent drawings. Working on a lovely sunny day in this beautiful part of the world is very special to me, and, the Lake District is on the doorstep of people like me, living in Low Furness.

There are, of course, 'ups and downs' in my line of work, but all in all, I enjoy my life as a chimney sweep.

## Arthur Evans: 'A Happy Boyhood'

*Arthur Evans was born in Barrow in 1922 and speaks of a boyhood spent in the Cemetery Cottages. The Cemetery Cottages consist of three rows of terraced houses: Beech Street, Lime Street and Maple Street, situated in the Ormsgill district of Barrow. Arthur lived in Beech Street opposite Thomas Round and his family. On leaving Barrow Grammar School, he worked in various places: the Post Office, Glaxo, and the shipyard. He went to college in 1966 and taught till retirement age. He wrote articles for the* NW Evening Mail *for nearly fifty years on natural and Cumbrian history, sometimes under the pseudonym of Rowan. He also wrote for the* Westmorland Gazette *for twenty years. Arthur has a wife, Jean, and three sons. He was interviewed on 10 October 2006.*

The one thing I remember of the Cemetery Cottages as a child was that we were always hungry. I was lucky because my mother was a good cook and she used to go scrounging for food from all sorts of places. We had hens so we had a constant supply of eggs, and my dad had an allotment and grew lots of vegetables: Brussels sprouts, cauliflowers etc. We had bags of vegetables in the winter and eggs in the summer, as well as lettuce and tomatoes. However, a lot of the friends I grew up with were quite literally starving. One of my friends, called Billy, who lived nearby, was always hungry and I can remember his mother gave him 2*d* for a cream cake for his dinner. He used to come to our house scrounging eggs from my mother who felt sorry for him even though after a while this had to stop because Billy was begging too many eggs. After all, there were five of us in our family – my parents and a brother and a sister.

Billy and I used to go fishing, 'kebbin' for codling to the black hole which was a deep tidal pool at the north end of Walney Channel and we were firmly convinced it was bottomless and went down to hell itself – we were terrified. We would go in this leaky old boat, a twelve footer called *Marjorie* which was big and clumsy, as were the oars which I could hardly reach. Billy used to steer. The codling (the young cod) used to come in with the tide and as it went out, the fish got trapped in the black hole. They were lovely fish, about two pounds in weight. The other fish we loved were 'flatties' (flat fish). We had a long fishing line with a few hooks on the end with bobbles of silver paper bobbing up and down. When caught, these fish were skinned and boned. This was delicious food, especially to kids who were always hungry.

Every season seemed to provide us with different things to eat. My mother would buy a sheep's head, simmer it till you ended up with the skull, all the flesh falling off and the juices of the flesh would come out of it. You would be left with delicious soup. After straining the soup, the flesh would be taken and mixed with gelatine and put in a mould and you would end up with potted meat. My mother would get bones and make another type of soup. She used to teach some of the women in the street to cook. Some really poor women were forced to go to Barrow market on a Saturday night and wait till eight o' clock at night when a butcher sold off poor cuts of meat very cheaply. The day I really hated was

Arthur Evans being presented with a watch in 2001 after completing nearly fifty years of writing articles for the *Evening Mail*. His wife, Jean, is on his left, holding a bouquet.
The editor, Steve Brauner, is on his right. *(NW Evening Mail)*

Monday when we had leftovers for dinner. It was washing day and the back door was left open so it was as cold as charity. Mother was bad-tempered and we were glad to go back to school. Washing was hung out at the side of the streets and washing lines were jealously guarded and God help the woman who put her washing on the wrong line. However, washing was sometimes stolen from the lines by desperately poor women. The thieves were never discovered as the theft could not be proved.

The rent for the terraced cottages in Beech Street was eight or nine shillings a week and some people were always in arrears. The rent collectors had a terrible time trying to collect rent. Some tenants would crouch out of sight when they knew the rent collector was coming. One day I remember the rent man managed to get the door open and shouted 'RENT!' and a wit of an old woman answered 'SPENT!' On another occasion, a rent collector told a woman he was considering selling the house to her but her husband told her not to have it as she would have rates to pay.

Young people couldn't afford rented accommodation so they lived in the parlour with a bedroom upstairs, sharing a kitchen; a newly-married bride with her mother-in-law! Rows often took place. There was a shop on the corner called Hollis's. It sold everything: drawing pads, books to write in, slices of ham, tinned stuff, and beer (surreptitiously).

Going back to my friend Billy, I was told the following story: His life changed for the better when he joined the army. He thought he was in heaven because for the first time in his life he had several square meals a day, he slept in a trunk bed with lovely warm bed covers and he could have a shower whenever he wanted. This life, however, took a tragic turn when his regiment attacked the Germans for the final attack in the Second World War. Billy had only gone about twenty yards when he was killed by a sniper. His mates had looked after him and had become like fathers to him, making sure he was okay for he was such a genteel, lovely lad – innocence personified. Everybody liked him and when he was killed, they stormed the abandoned building where he died. This was a French chateau and all the furniture remained, including lovely bedding. Billy's friends wrapped poor Billy in silk sheets, dug a grave and buried him. I've never forgotten him.

There were those living in the Cemetery Cottages who were survivors but then there were those who just gave up and took to drink. To a boy like me, growing up in the Cemetery Cottages at this time was an enriching experience that stood me in good stead for the rest of my life. I learnt a lot about people for what they were, and that you didn't have to have money to be decent. It was a unique place.

# Sarah (Sally) McAuliffe: 'A Long Life'

*'My Auntie Sally', by Agnes Crayston, written in 2004 when Sarah (Sally) McAuliffe reached her 100th birthday.*

Auntie Sally was born in 1904 and is the last survivor of a family of nine brothers and sisters. Some of the family married and their children, grandchildren and great-grandchildren are around to remember her in her earlier days and to celebrate her long life. We are all made welcome when we visit her at Boarbank Hall where she now lives in the care of the Augustinian Sisters and their staff.

Our memories of this very versatile lady go back to our own early days when the McAuliffe family lived with their mother in Buccleuch Street, Barrow, after the early death of their father. The main thing about them as a family was their good humour. They must have been living in very cramped conditions until some of them married and moved into their own homes, and of course, it was quite a number of years later before we became aware of them, but they all seemed to get along well together and also with each others' in-laws. Auntie Sally played the piano, accompanying the others as they sang solos at family parties. A great variety of music was sung: ballads, opera, operetta and modern songs, including *Forces' Favourites* during the Second World War. Christmas was the main season for this and many quite active games were on the programme too. Sally was often the MC, making sure the rules were kept.

Most of my auntie's leisure activities were centred on St Mary's Church in Duke Street. She sang in the choir, was a member of the Concert Party and played principal parts in plays and operettas. Tennis and badminton were played with enthusiasm. The Girl Guide movement was a favourite pastime of hers, especially the outdoor activities. Holidays were taken all over the British Isles, and she travelled abroad on a number of occasions, sometimes to visit relatives in America, but also on pilgrimage to Lourdes, and to see the Passion Play in Oberammergau.

As the years passed, some of Auntie Sally's family became ill and she helped to care for them in hospital, sometimes in off the beaten track places, when necessary, and she worked full-time to provide an income and a comfortable home.

Auntie Sally's work as a seamstress is a story on its own. Apprenticed to Miss Barrow, one of the top tailoresses in the town, and subsequently through her work at May Duff's in Ulverston, Sally created legendary dresses, hats, suits and other outfits, not only for the quality who graced May Duff's establishment with their presence, but also on special occasions for family and friends. At that time, many society weddings and court presentations were dressed by May Duff; the detailed beading and other intricate work being sewn by hand. Some of the outfits had to be delivered to obscure addresses in the surrounding countryside and Auntie was sometimes the chosen messenger; a doubtful privilege. Those of us who had First Communion outfits, wedding dresses, ball gowns and fancy dress costumes made by Auntie Sally will never forget the special feeling we had wearing them. They always felt superior to anything else we wore, and as only the best materials were used, they never wore out.

Sally as a young woman in May Duff's garden. *(Morris family)*

During the war, Sally left May Duff's shop and came to work in Barrow at the trimming shop (Wrigley's), in Dalton Road. This did away with the journey to and from Ulverston, which had become quite hazardous in the blackout of the Second World War. However, as a member of staff, Auntie Sally was expected to take her turn at fire watching, usually on the roof of the building, so it wasn't exactly a safe haven.

After this period, Auntie Sally spent most of her working life as a seamstress in North Lonsdale Hospital. The regime at that time was that of a matron in charge of proceedings and Matron James was typically that. Auntie Sally's expertise was appreciated there and she stayed on until she was seventy, before retiring for a well earned rest…? Not a bit of it! She was a very active member of the Townswomen's Guild, including the choir and the drama group. Her wide experience of music and costume was very useful at that time. She aimed to improve her performance as a pianist, having music lessons when she was in her eighties, the better to accompany the choir on concerts for the 'old folk'. She was also one of the first

I am so pleased to know that you
are celebrating your one hundredth
birthday on 10th February, 2004.  I
send my congratulations and best
wishes to you on such a special
occasion.

*Elizabeth R*

Miss Sarah McAuliffe

Copy of telegram from
Queen Elizabeth II.

Barrovians to join the Civic Society, when the late Bill Rollinson was President.
Another of her interests was St John's Ambulance, of which she was a member for
several years.

With the help and cooperation of everyone at Boarbank, all generations of the
family have celebrated Auntie Sally's 100th birthday and lunch at Graythwaite
Manor Hotel. During an extended period of five days, Mass was said at Boarbank
and St Mary's Barrow, where some of the parishioners were able to join us. Two
birthday cakes were cut and Sally received the all important telegram from Queen
Elizabeth II, which had been talked about for months.

Sarah (Sally) McAuliffe at her 100th birthday party. Standing left to right: Grace Morris, Joe Morris, Michael McKeever, Jim Morris, Margery Morris, Agnes Crayston, Theresa Ruscillo, Anne Tunn, Anthony Ruscillo. Seated left to right: Kathleen Morris, Sally McAuliffe, Patricia McKeever, Nan Morris. *(NW Evening Mail)*

Later in the year, younger members of the family and some friends and parishioners joined us with Auntie Sally for Mass in St Mary's Church, the parish of which she was a member until recently. This was followed by lunch at the Glengarth Hotel, a great gathering, continuing our tradition of celebrating family events.

February 2007: Now very close to her 103rd birthday, Auntie Sally is still cared for at Boarbank. Less aware of the hustle and bustle of everyday life, she will certainly be galvanised into action when she realises there is birthday cake about.

*Miss Sarah McAuliffe died on 26 March 2007. Facts of her long life have been collated by various members of her family, her failing memory preventing a recording being made.*

# EIGHT

# PREACHING, TEACHING & LEARNING

## The Revd Allan Mitchell

*The Revd Allan Mitchell was born in Barrow in 1952. He has one sister and one brother, is married to Denise and has two children. Allan was educated locally: at Victoria Infant School, Victoria Junior School, the Technical School and Thorncliffe Comprehensive. He has been vicar of St Mary's Parish Church, Dalton, for the last eight years. Alan was interviewed 2 November 2006.*

I first realised I had a vocation to the ministry when I was ten or eleven; I had always been involved with St Matthew's Church in Barrow. Canon Bucks was the vicar and the rural dean of the area. There were then lots and lots of young curates being trained at the time under Canon Bucks, and they had a kind of strange influence over me; the very fact that young men were committing themselves to God in this way, and perhaps that's where the calling came from, because I was inspired by what they did and how they spoke and the words that they said. So when I was about ten or eleven I had this thought in me to be a clergyman and become ordained; that thought came and went over the secondary school years. At one time I thought I was going to be an illustrator and perhaps an art teacher; one time I thought strongly about going to college to learn more about gardening and horticulture, but the call came back continually. When I was about seventeen, I went for my first interview with the Church of England, with a bishop and lay people to Mary Sumner's house on the south coast and they interviewed me over a weekend to see if they could put me forward for ordination and they recommended me to Bishop Cyril Bully of the diocese of Carlisle, with the request that I should be ordained, and he kindly, with the advice of his archdeacons, said that I should find some place to be trained as a vicar.

When I left school, I could have gone to university or theological college but I went straight into becoming a member of a religious community, the Society of the Sacred Mission, which is the Kelham Fathers, and they lived in a village called Kelham which is just outside Newark in Nottinghamshire. I joined them when I was eighteen. Kelham was a time of learning for me both spiritually and academically, as well as in life's university. I stayed at Kelham for a good number of years. Prior to that, every summer, because my dad worked in the cemetery, I was employed as a gardener and labourer in Barrow cemetery; that's a job I've always got an affection for and I remember it well.

After leaving Kelham, I went back to gardening and labouring in Barrow cemetery and I worked there for two years. From the cemetery they moved me to Barrow Parks and that's when I became the lawnmower man and I used to cut all the grass verges in the town and the open public spaces. I thoroughly enjoyed that and I remember John Crossfield, the head gardener and others, and that made this a very happy time. When I was there, I found a wife, not in the cemetery or in the park, but elsewhere, and I got married to Denise in 1976 and that was the hottest summer on record, until this year [2006]. It was a good time. We got married at St Matthew's, Barrow; Denise was from St Luke's Church.

I completed my training for the ministry at Lincoln Theological College; I was there for eighteen months and I got my qualifications. The Bishop of Carlisle, who was then Bishop Halsey, wrote me a letter and extended an invitation for me to serve on the west coast in Whitehaven in a parish called St Peter's, Kells, where the only working mine in the county was in existence; it was the Haig Pit, which went under the Solway for three miles. So I was living in a mining community and that was a good experience for me, being part of such a hard working and industrious community on the west coast of Cumbria.

I haven't had any person shout anything at me or call me names and I have never encountered bigotry in any church in which I have served; I have always been welcomed. Those churches have mainly been on the west coast of Cumbria, at Whitehaven, Workington, Carlisle, Pennington, Lindal, Marton and Swarthmoor and now of course, Dalton-in-Furness.

I have now been vicar of St Mary's Parish Church, Dalton for eight years – going into my ninth year in 2007. I came here as vicar of one parish and now I am vicar of another parish which has become a combined unit, so we are now Dalton and Ireleth with Askam. There is a possibility of grouping even more parishes: Grizebeck and Kirkby and Urswick, Aldingham, Rampside and Dendron in the next eighteen months, so it will become quite a large grouping of different churches, of which the vicar of Dalton will be the team leader.

Next year we will be having some special celebrations to mark the twentieth anniversary of the founding of the ecumenical movement; it was initially called the LEP – a local ecumenical partnership. Within the different denominations in the area: the Roman Catholic Church, the United Reform Church, the Methodist Church and the Christian Fellowship groups in the town, there are good relationships and in Dalton, we were the first ecumenical project to be formed. The strength of ecumenism depends on the church leaders, and without their help, I don't think very much would go on.

I am often asked if congregational numbers are increasing or decreasing. I always look at my numbers at the different services in the church and I believe they are holding their own. I say that because over a twelve-month period, I probably bury or cremate fifty per cent of my congregation and working on that kind of assessment, church numbers should have decreased, but in actual fact, we always get people in to fill the empty pews that are left. The numbers over the years have maintained their capacity in all the different services. On special occasions, we can attract large numbers: Christmas, Easter, Harvest and other events and celebrations. As for Sunday worship, and mid-week worship, the numbers have actually gone up over the last eight years.

*Christenings, weddings and funerals – a vicar's lot. Allan Mitchell remembers some memorable ones.*

I was looking at the books just last weekend – up to now, in 2006, we've done seventy-two christenings, and we've probably got another twelve or thirteen to do before the end of the year. I have bookings for a christening for May 2007 already! I can recall one memorable christening that took place at Pennington. The child, who was a toddler, took an immediate dislike to me; one of the parents was a doctor, the other a nurse. I said there and then that I wasn't going to pick up the child, and dad would have to hold her, which he did. However, she wriggled and wriggled all through the service and wasn't very happy at all, and it was impossible to pour the water over the head, so I splashed the water and Dad got more water on him than the child did, on the brow. Everyone seemed to get drenched – it was good fun.

I have thirty weddings planned for next year and this year I have done about twenty-two. I always remember a wedding I took in Carlisle; the groom was in the army and the girl was in her late teens and from the city and she could talk and talk and talk and he would never say anything. He was very, very shy – very quiet, but she could talk for England. I knew she was expecting because her physical condition had altered over the months when we had been preparing for the wedding, having our talks. On the actual wedding day she came in and waddled down the aisle – he stood there at attention in his uniform, never moved, never said anything. When we'd done the actual vows and promises, the bride, having spoken for him as much as she could: 'I do, I will, he has done,' I gave the nuptial blessing. She got up and started to sway from side to side. I thought the stiletto heel of her shoe had caught in the hem of her dress, but that wasn't the case. She fainted and as she went down, Dad, who was in the front pew, got up immediately and grabbed her shoulders and the two ushers who were her brothers and who must have been in training for Carlisle United at the time, ran down the centre aisle and grabbed an ankle each, and they said, 'Vicar, we'll just take her into the vestry and revive her.' At that point they lifted her up. Now, in those days the fashion was to have hoops in the hems of wedding dresses; as she was lifted, the hoop moved with her, moved over her body and got stuck on her tum, because she was heavily pregnant; you could see everything borrowed, new and blue. The young bride did actually come round after drinking a drop of rum that Dad provided. We signed the registers and it all worked out well. The couple not only had that baby but several more children since that year, and sometimes, when I'm in Carlisle, I bump into the happy family and they remember their memorable wedding day very well.

This year there have been about 170 funerals. They are not all in church, for some are at the crematorium chapel. I do tend to remember all of them. One very

The Revd Allan Mitchell
officiating at the funeral
of Ivor Kelland.
(NW Evening Mail)

memorable funeral took place recently, that of Ivor Kelland. His funeral service was
a very large one because in many respects he was a larger than life man and he
touched the lives of so many different people; we had over 800 people in church to
pay their respects and to give him a good send-off. I remember the two gentlemen
who paid the tributes; they had the place rolling in laughter as they talked about
Ivor and his exploits, not just on the sport's field but in the local hostelries of the
area, as he travelled up to the west coast to train some of the lads up there, and as a
reporter and a broadcaster for Radio Cumbria as well.

The other service was for a father and son, the Rushtons, who had died in Morecambe Bay when the tide came in. To have a father and his child laying side by side in coffins in the one service is an occasion that I will never forget.

## The Annual Christmas Tree Festival

One day in the year 2000, a gentleman from Canada joined our congregation and he told me about an exhibition of Christmas trees he had seen in Canada. The trees had been designed by professional artists, sculptors and designers and they were in a museum in Vancouver. He said they looked splendid, and that was what gave me the idea for the people to decorate and design trees. In the first year we managed to get the groups and organisations and schools in the town involved and twenty-seven trees were decorated. This year there will be fifty-four trees: twelve at Askam in Duddon Road Methodist Church, and the rest in the parish church. The Tree Festival has grown and it now takes a high priority in peoples' diaries for Christmas. We celebrate Christmas really very early as the Festival runs from the first of December through to the sixth of January. This year it's starting on the first of December with a pantomime procession through the town, and we have invited the school children to dress up in pantomime characters; we have a horse and carriage to take Cinderella and Snow White through the town. The mayors of the area have been invited to celebrate with us. The Tree Festival will hopefully get stronger and stronger as the years go by. The overall theme this year is 'A Moment in Time'.

In ten years' time I will be coming up to retiring age, but whether I will be retiring from Dalton or not depends, not on me, but the calling that God gives to me. I usually set out five-year plans when I am in a parish and as I have been here eight years, moving into my ninth year, two five years will bring me to a tenth year here and then the thought of moving to another parish might come to mind. There are a few conditions that surround moving such as whether the parish you are moving from is ready for you to leave. There are questions to be asked: 'Is there a challenge, is there an opportunity still here in the community to do things, will the people still be willing, able and enthusiastic to work with me?'

I might think I've done enough and can't do any more and then start looking for another place to go. However, that decision depends on the bishop and a number of factors within the diocese; it also depends on where the family is, and what they are hoping to do, to achieve. If I did move, it would be nice to stay in the diocese and go back to the west coast.

## Jennifer Billingham

*Jennifer Billingham (née Liddell), was born in 1948 in Barrow. She was educated at South Walney Primary School and Barrow Grammar School for Girls. She is married to Frank, a former Barrow rugby player, and has one nineteen-year-old student son called Jack – the first ever Jack to be born at Risedale Maternity Home, Barrow. She has recently retired from her position as Head Teacher at Sandside School, near Ulverston-in-Furness, where she had taught for forty years. Jennifer was interviewed on 29 August 2006.*

I always knew I wanted to work with children, but I wasn't quite sure whether it was nursing or teaching. I became aware of children with learning disabilities when I was about thirteen or fourteen. My mother used to visit the George Hastwell Centre, a school for children with severe learning disabilities in Barrow, and I sometimes went with her, and I also had a friend at the grammar school who had a brother who had Down's syndrome. I think this was what motivated me to work with children with learning difficulties.

Then I heard of Sandside which was then a training centre; the original Sandside School had been built at the turn of the century to educate the children who lived in the area of Ulverston; it was the primary school. I seemed to have been in the right place at the right time for an opportunity arose. There was an advertisement in the paper just after I left the grammar school for a young person to go and work at Sandside. Then, Lancashire County Council, as it was then, offered to pay me to go to train to teach, providing I came back and worked there for a minimum of two years.

Consequently I returned to Sandside after university and when the two years were up, I stayed because there was so much that needed to be done. It became quite a challenge, and I felt I needed to be there to do whatever it took to accept the challenge. When I first went to Sandside there were ten children in each class and three classes; now there are ten classes and over fifty staff and that includes dinner ladies. There are a high number of classroom support assistants. The children start at two and go on till they are nineteen years old.

The majority of the children have Down's syndrome and therefore severe learning disabilities, a number have severe physical difficulties, often as a result of a brain injury at birth; some are blind or deaf. The biggest increase in recent years for whatever reason, has been those children with autism and that has been quite overwhelming.

In the forty years I've been teaching at Sandside, people must have said to me thousands of times, 'You must be very patient.' I'm not convinced I am a very patient person, but perhaps I am, but it doesn't mean being patient with the children when they are difficult, but patiently waiting for them to achieve the next step and that can take years. As well as patience, to teach children with severe learning difficulties, you've got to be inventive because you've got to try and teach the same concept in all kinds of different ways, even to fastening shoe laces, and you've got to have bags of common sense.

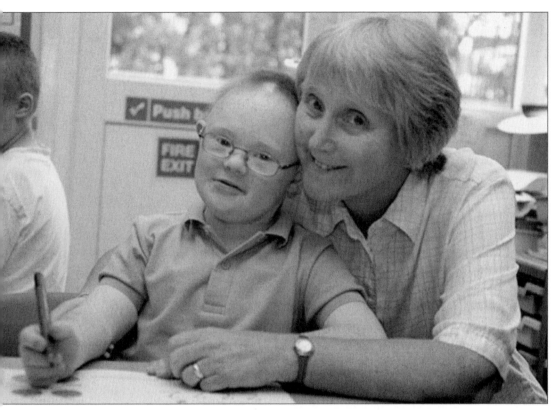

Jennifer Billingham with her pupil, Joshua Botham, who at the time was nine years old.
(*NW Evening Mail*)

Originally in the 1960s the school had very poor resources in terms of teaching aids and I made a lot of things myself, and looking back I suspect a number of those youngsters were very bored, but we were very limited by what was available in school. The opposite is the case now. We have a computer suite with ten PCs and a number of laptops, interactive white boards, webcams, video conferencing and a library. Children from mainstream schools, who have failed for whatever reason, are often taken in at Sandside and they have been used to such facilities. It has certainly improved the lot of all the pupils.

During my forty years at Sandside, there have been sad, happy and humorous moments. The saddest moments have always been when children have died in our care or at home. Many of these children have got life-threatening conditions; I can remember losing six or seven children and that's always a terrible time. However, there were thousands of happy times; perhaps the happiest was when we won yet another fight to keep the school open. The year before I became head I'd been deputy and my predecessor had been away on a course for a year and indicated he wouldn't be returning, and I was asked to be acting head while, and I quote, 'the future of the school was determined.'

At that point, which would have been 1979, there were only twenty children in the school and it was a fairly expensive school to run and people were trying to say that it was no longer financially viable. I don't think that the powers that be had reckoned on the support that there would be. I formed a small committee, not only of the great and the good, but good, hard working parents who believed in the school and we formed a very good strategy; we went into the town and collected signatures for which we had no problem. We organised a public meeting in support of the school which we opened to the general public and particularly to former pupils of the school, not only to those with learning difficulties, but those who had attended the school in the '20s, '30s and '40s. It was unbelievable the number of those who turned up; some had come from away and we couldn't fit them all in the school so they had to stand in the classroom with open doors. They sent two people from the Education Authority and I must say the audience was patient and I said, 'Please let them speak, let them give what they think is their case for closure.' They could hardly get out of the door, the support was so overwhelming and it wasn't just sentimental, it was support based on success, i.e. based on the success of the pupils in the school and the good will we had engendered. That happened another couple of times and each time we did similar things with satisfactory results so those were happy times. I believe the school is secure now or I probably wouldn't have retired at this time. And, we've had lots and lots of fun with the children.

There have also been lots of humorous times and one in particular. I was showing some students around the school; they were training to teach. There was quite a group of them and I was speaking to them in the staff room which had an open door leading to the corridor and one of them asked, 'What do you feel your most recent success has been?' I pointed out a boy in the playground and I said until recently his language had been appalling but I'd worked really hard to try to get across to him not to swear so badly; really I was patting myself on the back. At that moment it started to rain really heavily and I heard the children coming in and the boy at the front shouted, 'It's bloody well pissing it down out there!' So I said, 'Don't ever rest on your laurels, girls, or you will be made a fool of.'

Outsiders might mistakenly think that play-time for Sandside is different from play-time in mainstream schools but it isn't. We left the old Victorian building in 1998 because we were just too big for it and we moved into the adjacent building which had been the Adult Training Centre for adults with learning difficulties. They moved into the town and that building was refurbished for us and we moved into it in September 1997 and we very quickly outgrew that building as well and had a very big extension built on the side which John Hutton opened in 2001. So the new block is Upper School, Year Seven and the other building is from Nursery to Year Six; both buildings have their own play areas, so the nursery has a little purpose-built play dale and the infants and juniors have a very long playground at the back, and at the moment a sensory play ground is being created. The older children have a big playground at the front and they've got basketball and football nets.

Just as in mainstream schools, assemblies are held; there's one school assembly on Fridays but the classes have little assemblies and little prayers on other days. Friday afternoon assembly will have a main topic, for instance, when it was Remembrance

Day, I used to get a box of poppies from the British Legion and I talked to the children about why we remember, and those children who could read, and there are quite a lot of those, would download poems from the internet about Flanders Field. A nice service would follow and the children would then sing very loudly, something with a religious theme. At the end of this assembly I used to stand at the door and give every child a poppy and it was amazing to see eighty-two children with severe disabilities leave that hall in silence, remembering as best they could those who had died for their country. It's important that they should know about part of their history.

*Jennifer invited Alice Leach to Furness Abbey, around 1994, to join her and ten of her pupils in a walk round the abbey.*

At that time I was teaching RE, which isn't the easiest subject to teach children who are often devoid of imagination and who find it difficult to think historically; to them history might be what they had for breakfast this morning, geography might be the way they go home on the mini-bus or where they went on their holidays, or what they see as they pass. I was trying to make history come alive for them and I've always been interested in the abbey and thought it was such a fantastic resource for schools. The children thought it was wonderful to get dressed up in the monks' habits. They liked looking in the museum as well. I was, as always, surprised not only by their good behaviour which is often remarked on, but how they concentrated on what Alice Leach was telling them, and it isn't easy to get to that level; they understood as well as they could and asked some questions. They loved the part of the abbey where the monks used to sing and I can see little Helen now; (we couldn't find a habit small enough for her). She looked up to the sky and shouted, 'Hello God, are you there, God?' She had understood what she had been told. Then we moved on to where the monks used to wash their hands and they thought it was cool that the monks did not have regular baths. Walking around, seeing them in a line. That was a great day!

During my time at Sandside, I was nearly always satisfied that most children had reached their potential. We had two Ofsted inspections while I was there and the report stated that the children had made remarkable progress from a very poor start. I think those children who did not achieve their potential were some of those children with autism who were just not able to learn effectively because autism gets in the way of learning and they can't always take advantage of learning opportunities.

When the children leave school to start work, options have always been limited, although I think they are widening; ten years ago the majority would go to a day centre such as Mill Lane or Furness and Cartmel Day Services, whereas now, more and more are going to either residential colleges that might be run by Mencap or the Lindeth College at Windermere, which takes students from the age of nineteen for three years to give them independence and training, and a number go to Furness College. I think my concern particularly for those that go away, is what happens to them when they come back, for the majority are not employable, and quite often they have to start fighting for a place at the day centre, which they would have got automatically if they had gone there at nineteen.

The biggest blot on my landscape was that I always felt that there were people looking over their shoulders and keeping an eye on us because we were situated between George Hastwell School in Barrow and the Sandgate School at Kendal. I think they thought that maybe we were not necessary, but the school takes children from a vast catchment area including Ravenglass, Windermere and Millom. There was just nowhere else for those children to have gone. It's been a long, hard fight, but I do think the battle has been won.

Parents have always been very supportive and this is very gratifying. I've always known they appreciated my efforts and the efforts of the staff from letters that they've written and comments they have made at face to face meetings that I had with them. However, when I retired, I was amazed when I received 370 cards and an incredible number of letters from parents. I haven't been able to read them all yet because of the final assembly; many of those attending were very very distressed, so I've still to tackle the box of cards and letters. The support has been overwhelming.

I think in future years, Sandside School will serve the community in quite different ways. It is already a centre of excellence, but I think it will be used more by teachers from mainstream schools who are doing their best to include some of these children in their schools, and who are struggling. I think they will come to the school, (they often do now), but I think their numbers will increase. Sandside has an inclusion officer who will go out to schools to assist, because the school does not have elastic walls and while it has what the majority of parents want, who have a child like this, it isn't what they all want. Many of them want mainstream school and for some, it works.

I think given the amount of equipment we've got, we might almost become a lending library of resources. I think the staff will offer training to the staff of other schools. That's great, but they must not forget that they are there first and foremost for their own pupils, some of whose parents have had to fight to get them in; that's what the school is about. My starting point was always 'What does this child really need?' I would hate the teachers to lose sight of that.

Everyone has been asking me about my plans for retirement. I've already been approached by a number of schools to help them with children whose learning difficulties are so significant that the school can't see how best they might access the curriculum. I feel a great need to go back to working with children rather than working with paper; that's really why I retired. When John Hutton said, 'I don't know why you are retiring, you are still needed here,' I replied, 'John, as long as your government keeps sending countless, unnecessary pieces of paper, good head teachers will go'. He accepted that and he brought me some House of Commons chocolates and champagne, which I enjoyed.

# NINE

# CHILDREN'S VOICES

*Vanessa Allen interviewed two of her pupils from Dane Ghyll School on 29 November 2006. Their names are Daniel Eccles and Georgia Drew. Both were then nine years old and both were born at Furness General Hospital, Barrow.*

## Daniel Eccles

I attended Hindpool Nursery before starting school. I can remember play-time and the sandpit. Luke went to the same school as me. When I first went into the classroom I remember where we put our coats and book bags. I liked going on the tricycles outside. I enjoy play-time most about school. I like playing football in the

Play-time at Dane Ghyll School. *(Vanessa Allen)*

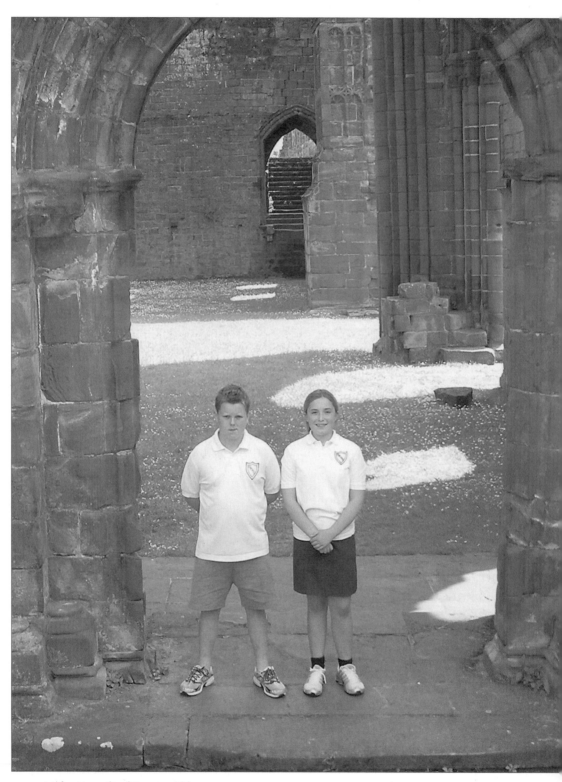

In the grounds of Furness Abbey.

summer on the field or with the playground equipment and playing on the basketball court. I play with my friends, Ross and Luke who are in my class. I think our playground equipment is good considering it's only a small school; we've got everything: football, rugby, playground equipment. I like the old equipment where you can go down the slide and the monkey bars.

At lunchtime I usually have a school dinner, but I'm having a packed lunch now. I like chicken slices with crackers, a yoghurt and a banana. We get three-quarters of an hour usually to eat our dinner, but infants go in at twelve o'clock and there's some spaces in the hall, so then we go in, one class at a time. On wet play-times we have a book where we can draw things and we swap cards. At the moment it's Shoot Out cards and Dr Who cards. There's about 360 cards in the Shoot Out book and 247 in the Doctor Who book. The rarest ticket is the golden ticket and I've nearly completed the Shoot Outs – I just need six. When you want to swap, if there's a dead good card like a five star shiny, you swap a few three star shiny cards. The best players are shiny and have the most stars. You swap cards with anyone who wants to swap. Doctor Who is all the go at the moment because of the TV programme.

Now I am one of the oldest pupils in the school. I think respect and manners are most important, especially in front of the younger ones and showing a good example.

If I could put five things into a time capsule, I would put in balls – I can't get away from them, like footballs, tennis balls, basketballs, rugby balls, cricket balls. If I could only put one ball in, it would probably be a football, because I love football and I play for a local team, Furness Rovers. I'm goalkeeper and we played our B team and won last week 3–0. Our highest win is 16–0. I've been playing for probably about three years and we go to train indoors at Thorncliffe School in the winter and in the summer we practise outdoors at our field. Football is really what I enjoy playing.

I would also put in a family photo and there's a nice one where my dad got his degree at the university. He's opening his degree and he's in his gown. I was about seven then. On the photo there's my mum, my dad, and me. My brother wasn't there then.

Some food would go in because food will all probably change. It would be adverts. I'd probably choose potatoes.

I'd put in a picture of my little brother because he wasn't on the other one. I like a picture of him when we were down in Devon and he's on the beach with his swim shorts on and the water was pretty cold, but then it started warming up. He went in and ran out, so we took a picture of him.

Lastly I would put a book in the time capsule like *Captain Underpants and The Wrath of the Wicked Wedgie Woman*. It's dead funny. I enjoy those books.

My hobbies are different sports; I like playing football, tennis, basketball, rugby and golf. I also like swimming; in fact, anything to do with sport.

My favourite shop is BL Sports in town; it's near the Coffee Bean. It has everything in it, like juice bottles, football boots, rugby boots. My dad bought some basketball boots and I'd like a basketball for Christmas. A basketball is usually bouncier than a football but if you kick it, it goes out of shape. I probably go to this shop about once a month.

I like playing games on computers. My uncle's got a dead good game called *Battlefield Two*. It's like a bit of a war game where you go from bases and you get tanks and bombs. Loads of people in the world go on this game and you're all playing against each other, unless you're on the same team. There's a Chinese Team and a Greek Team. There's helicopters and jets and vehicles. I probably play on my computer about an hour a week, but I also do computer lessons at school for about an hour a week.

We visit lots of places like the Dock Museum and Gummer's How. I like going on the boat on Lake Windermere; it's like a cruise ship. You can sit out in the summer and have your dinner on it. You can go shopping at Bowness. We don't visit that often because it's quite a long way away in the car because you've got to go round the lake to Bowness. My mum likes shopping there because there's nice shops. I've been to Gummer's How as well, it's a big hill and about half a year ago, me and my mum, dad and John Paul climbed it. Josh Jones was at the top of it with his family. There was a bit of fog but you could see Lake Windermere and Lakeside Hotel.

We usually go on holiday even if it's just to my Auntie Sam's in Newcastle. We stay at the Holiday Inn there. There's a big garden centre and my nanna and my mum like going there. There's a huge play-park – it's dead good and we all play on there while Mum and Nanna are watching. There's a little café where we have our lunch. They are coming to see us at Christmas.

In the summer holidays I think we're going to Disneyland, Paris. Last year we went to Devon. We stayed at an apartment, all to ourselves, self-catering. There was a beach literally right in front of our apartment, about twenty yards away. You just had to walk across the road and there was the beach. I did skimming boards: you throw it along the sea and you jump onto it and glide across the water. The beaches are sandy and cleaner than ours.

I think there are a few things I would like to change about Barrow. I would make more Sports' Centres and a few more places to go like the Play Zone and Lazer Zone. That's where you put these tags on and you try and shoot people. You win points and the person with the most points at the end of the game, wins. You shoot them with a laser gun and their gun stops for a few seconds and then it goes. You can shoot these things on the wall, but if it can see you while it's on, it makes you lose points. If you shoot so many times you can win things like gems and invisibility. There's lights like lights on a disco. I've been about five times, including parties. It's a party place. The Play Zone is for up to about age eight or ten, depending how tall you are. There's something for everybody. Mum and Dad usually have a coffee and sit about talking.

When I grow up I would like to be a famous footballer and play for Man United. They're my favourite team. I'm going on the 6 December, hopefully. They're playing Benfica and they've got to win. If they don't win they're out of the Champions' League. I've seen Fulham play Man United and I've seen West Ham when there was the George Best tribute and we all held posters up. I've never seen him play but I've seen all the clips that he was a great player – a great finisher.

My job might command me to go and live in Manchester or a big city, but my heart would still be in Barrow. I grew up here and I like it.

In ten years' time I think Barrow will be more modern and up to date. There'll be more things for the kids and more sports. There'll be lots more houses, I think and it will be a busier town.

## Georgia Drew

Before I started school I went to Bram Longstaffe Nursery on Barrow Island. I played with my friend called Madison and we played dolls in the playhouse. I can remember the first day when I started school, walking in and there were lots of faces staring at me I did not know many of those children when I started but it was nice coming to Dane Ghyll School when I was just four, being with my teacher and being comforted by other pupils of the school.

The things I enjoy most about our school are our lessons. My favourite lessons are Maths and Science. I like working with numbers and I've liked finding out about the earth, sun and moon every Wednesday in the Science lesson.

At play-times we sometimes go on the equipment and play on the wobbly bridge and the slides. Sometimes we play basketball with the basketballs and practise our shooting. Sometimes we just walk around talking. In the summer we're allowed to go and play on the grass and we're allowed to play football. We always look for ladybirds in the grass, because when they cut the grass, we make kind of nests for them to go in. Me and my friends, we play with the reception children so they don't feel scared because there's lots of older children around them. Sometimes I play with my two best friends, Lorna and Abbie.

At lunch-time I have a school dinner. My favourite is probably pasta and Bolognese sauce. Sometimes we have naan bread with it, and for pudding, normally we have some fruit or a yoghurt, or sometimes we can have a doughnut or a cookie. Sometimes there's only a little number stay for school dinners and sometimes, there's quite a big number. It tends to change in the winter and the summer, because people like hot dinners in the winter, but in the summer you're allowed to sit outside with your packed lunch. Then I have tuna sandwiches, a piece of fruit, a yoghurt, and sometime my mum lets me have a chocolate biscuit.

I am now one of the oldest children in the school and I think it is important to show smaller children how to react and giving them an example to show how you should act in school. In assembly we show them how to go out quietly and put your hand up in class and not to talk. We did a book for the reception children and everyone in the class did a little poster to go into the book. My poster was called 'Look after your own belongings' and there was a picture of coat hangers with coats and bags on the pegs.

If I could put five things into a time capsule they would be: probably my favourite book that I've read a lot. I've just finished reading *Friend and Foe* by Michael Morpurgo and I think that would be a good book to put in. There's a great story line. David and Tucky are the two main characters and always stick together as friends. Because they are evacuees, they have to go to live with a man called Mr Reynolds. They get up to all sorts because they have to start at a new school and get used to a new environment. The war went on for such a long time so this would have to be the new routine. I'd also probably put in my two favourite lesson books: my Maths and Science books from Year Five; probably these two because as I said before, they are my favourite lessons. Number three would be a bracelet my best friend got me when I started school here at Dane Ghyll. She's called Lorna. There's a lot of other things, so it would be hard to choose, but those three definitely.

I have several hobbies; I like playing netball because I'm in the netball team. My sister and I always go horse riding every Saturday over at Seaview [Biggar Village, Walney Island]. I like swimming for fun because it's really good fun going under the water. I go to Dalton Leisure Centre with my sister. She's eleven and goes to Dowdales Secondary School. My mum drops us off and pays us in. Then we just go and have a swim. Then she'll come and pick us up at a certain time. I also go swimming with school and we have lessons with Mr Heaton [the coach]. We all go there with Mrs Allen [Year Five teacher].

When I go to town shopping I always like going in Ottakar's [now Waterstone's] to get a book. I go through quite a lot of books, so my mum sometimes lets me go in there and get a new book to read.

I like going on computers to find out facts. Besides that, there's games and you can get programmes for your work. If you go into Google on the internet, you can find out almost everything for Science homework; you could either go on Google and type Science or Moon or whatever you're learning about. Then if you click, it gives you a big sheet with lots of facts.

I often visit places close to Barrow like Ulverston, because my auntie lives there. We go to the Lake District every summer and we go camping up in Coniston because my dad has a friend up there who owns a big field, so we camp out there. I like camping because you get out in the fresh air and sometimes my dad lets us go and paddle on Coniston Water. Sometimes we put on our swimsuits but we're not allowed to go further than a couple of yards away from the shore. I like all the little shops at Coniston and we go out on the boat trips. Sometimes we go to Grasmere to the Gingerbread Shop.

I remember going on holiday to Cornwall in the summer. We went boogie boarding and my dad had a try out at surfing but he wasn't very good! For boogie boarding you get your board, go a little bit away from the shore and you wait for a wave. You lay down on your tummy and the wave brings you back along to the shore. We stayed in a caravan. My dad went to a surfing class, where you practised on a stand and then the teacher took him into the water. He had a go on the waves, but he wasn't very good – he kept falling over.

I think there are plenty of things in Barrow for children of my age. There's quite a lot of parks and there's lots of entertainment. There's lots of history in Barrow like Furness Abbey. We've got the cinema and bowling. We don't go that often to the cinema. Sometimes we have to wait for a film to come out on DVD or video and then we're allowed to get it to play on the DVD player at home.

If I could change anything about Barrow it would probably be littering on the floor, because lots of people throw chewing gum on the floor and it would be a lot nicer if people stopped doing that.

When I grow up I would like to study law. I think I'd be the first person to do that in my family. I'll have to go to senior school and university to study the law and then I'd be a lawyer. For the job I'd like to do I would have to move away from Barrow to go to university. I like Cornwall, but I would have thought there would be a lot more opportunities in London. I don't know yet, because I wouldn't like to be that far away from my family. My grandma has lots of relatives in Scotland.

In ten years' time I think Barrow will be a lot more popular than it is at the moment. I think it might get a lot bigger than it is. There might be a lot more building work and I think it will grow with a lot more population.

If I had the opportunity to go into BAE Systems and to be there when a submarine is actually launched, I think it would be great, for I've never actually seen

The Duchess of Cornwall meets some local school children. The boys in the jumpers with badges are from St George's C of E Primary School. *(BAE Systems Submarine Solutions, Barrow-in-Furness)*

The Duchess of Cornwall launching the submarine *Astute*. Murray Easton, Managing Director of BAE Systems is on her left. *(BAE Systems Submarine Solutions, Barrow-in-Furness)*

a submarine being launched before and I'd like to go. I think that would be very exciting and interesting if we could do that next year in 2007.

*Georgia got her wish and on Friday 8 June 2007, Year Five from Dane Ghyll School, along with some other local schools, went to BAE to see the launch of HMS* Astute. *Georgia made the following comments:*

It was a great honour because Camilla, Duchess of Cornwall launched the *Astute*; it was a great experience and I shall never forget it. My favourite part of the launch was when Camilla smashed a bottle of home-brewed beer against the submarine.